Teacher Leadership in Mathematics and Science

Casebook and Facilitator's Guide

Barbara Miller

Jean Moon

Susan Elko

with

Deborah Bryant Spencer

HEINEMANN
Portsmouth, NH

HEINEMANN
A division of Reed Elsevier Inc.
361 Hanover Street
Portsmouth, NH 03801–3912
www.heinemann.com

Offices and agents throughout the world

Library of Congress Cataloging-in-Publication Data
Miller, Barbara
  Teacher leadership in mathematics and science : casebook and facilitator's guide / Barbara Miller, Jean Moon, Susan Elko, with Deborah Bryant Spencer.
    p. cm.
  Includes bibliographical references and index.
  ISBN 0-325-00327-0 (alk. paper)
  1. Mathematics teachers—Training of—United States—Case studies.   2. Science teachers—Training of—United States—Case studies.   3. Educational leadership—United States—Case studies. I. Moon, Jean.   II. Elko, Susan.   III. Title.

QA13 .M53 2000
510.7'1073—dc21

00–044982

Editor: Leigh Peake
Production: Sonja S. Chapman
Cover design: Jenny Jensen Greenleaf
Manufacturing: Deanna Richardson

Printed in the United States of America on acid-free paper

04   03   02   01   VP   2   3   4   5

CONTENTS

FOREWORD

Teacher leadership may be the most difficult challenge facing today's education reform initiatives. Teachers, prepared to work with young people and often accomplished in that role, are being asked to assume leadership roles at an ever-increasing rate. Yet, unlike businesses who often invest heavily in building new skills in the employees they promote to leadership positions, our education systems most often leave teachers to sink or swim, as they face new jobs as coaches, trainers, and facilitators for those who were their peers just yesterday.

This book is a godsend for those who prepare and support teacher leaders. It provides well-structured materials that can help build a wide variety of skills, understandings, and dispositions required for teachers to play optimal leadership roles. And it helps new teachers begin to answer the following questions:

- How do I work with resistant teachers?
- How do I give constructive feedback to my neighbor teacher?
- How can I get the principal's support?
- How can we stretch our existing resources, and how can we use them to maximize our impact?

Professional development for teacher leaders, like professional development for teachers in general, is in the midst of a transformation. For more than a decade, educators have acknowledged that learning takes place in many ways, and that, consequently, professional development should take many different forms. Yet the one-time inservice workshop or institute has persisted as the primary vehicle for learning. This book, however, breaks that mold by using a strategy long-valued for preparing lawyers and doctors: the case method. Through the discussion of cases, professionals "live" the dilemmas and situations encountered in their field. As noted in this book, cases give them a window to view the practice of others and a mirror to reflect on their own.

This book uses cases to illuminate many of the dilemmas faced day-to-day by teacher leaders, both novice and veteran. The cases are vivid and rich—real to all who serve in leadership roles. They are written in such a way that they can stimulate discussions, deepen thinking, and challenge easy solutions to common problems.

However, this is more than a casebook. It is a detailed guide to facilitating case discussions in a way that models effective professional development. It helps the facilitator determine which cases are the most appropriate for participants, lead the discussion from description to analysis to reflection, and guide participants in searching carefully for application to their own practice. Suggested activities engage participants with each other as they come to understand different approaches to common dilemmas as well as analyze the consequences of different solutions. The discussions can take several paths, with engaging initiation and closure activities.

This casebook represents lessons learned from some of the most thoughtful action research that has been conducted in the area of teacher leadership. Not only do the cases result from the authors' extensive work with teacher leaders in a number of challenging science and mathematics reform initiatives, they also have been tested with groups of teacher leaders in order to develop discussion activities that have the most impact on the practice of the participants.

Meaningful, well-crafted materials for use with teacher leaders are few and far between. These cases and the accompanying guides for facilitating discussion are both conceptually sound and remarkably practical. The reader of this book can have confidence that their use will create more thoughtful, knowledgeable, and confident teacher leaders—whose visions and abilities have gone beyond those required for educating young people to those that will help transform the practice of teachers of science and mathematics.

—Susan Loucks-Horsley

PREFACE

Teacher leadership is a feature of many efforts to reform classrooms, schools, and districts. Yet, there are few clear and shared images of teacher leaders in action, nor are there many materials to support the development of teacher leaders. We see this casebook on teacher leadership as meeting both those needs. The materials identify the dilemmas that teacher leaders face as they engage in their work and highlight the capacities that teacher leaders need to be effective in their roles. We offer seven compelling pictures of teacher leaders engaged in mathematics and science reform and provide resources to aid in the development of teacher leaders.

These cases and facilitation materials grew out of two reform projects in which teacher leaders are key players, and the stories of the development of these materials are recounted below. These materials have been "repurposed" and expanded to fit together in this volume, a collaborative effort by three institutions: Merck Institute for Science Education, ExxonMobil Foundation (at the time, Exxon Education Foundation), and Education Development Center.

The Merck Institute for Science Education (MISE, see p. 147) developed and contributed the cases on science leadership issues. Merck & Co, Inc. created the Institute in 1993 to improve student performance and participation in science. To achieve these goals, MISE focuses on building teachers' capacity by providing professional development programs for K–8 science teachers in four districts adjacent to major Merck facilities. The keystone of these professional development programs is the Leader Teacher Institute (LTI), a three-year program designed to deepen teachers' content knowledge, strengthen their teaching practice, and build their leadership skills. Through inquiry, teachers learn science by doing science and use this experience to transform science learning in their classrooms. Woven into the teachers' investigations of science are methods for engaging all children and for determining student understanding of important science content. Teachers also actively construct ways to integrate mathematics, literature, and technology into science. In addition, Leader Teachers develop skills for instructing and coaching colleagues and for advocating standards-based practice to parents and the community.

The cases on leadership in science were developed in response to a need perceived in the LTI by Susan Elko, who was at that time MISE's Manager of Professional Development Programs. Leader Teachers were struggling to define how they could function as leaders beyond their classroom teacher roles. Elko found that using a case offered

Leader Teachers a way to express their concerns about playing a leadership role and identify skills they needed to develop. This response led to a collaboration between Elko and Barbara Miller and Deborah Bryant Spencer at Education Development Center to develop three new cases, each one focusing on a particular leadership role played by Leader Teachers: coach of peers, instructor of colleagues, and advocate of systemic education reform. The cases feature characters functioning in similar settings with similar dilemmas as those identified in interviews with MISE's Leader Teachers and school administrators.

Multiple purposes were considered in framing the MISE cases. The most obvious was to create models of teachers functioning as coaches, instructors, and advocates, and to raise issues common to teacher leaders in these roles. A less obvious, but equally important, purpose was to help Leader Teachers develop effective communication skills. Thus the dialogue in the cases was written to complement the communication skills component of the LTI. Participants used these materials to analyze the challenges of teacher leadership, to pinpoint their personal hopes and fears associated with a new level of responsibility in systemic science education reform, and to strategize about how they might be more effective in their leadership roles.

The ExxonMobil Foundation (see p. 144), dedicated to strengthening education, especially in mathematics, science, and engineering, developed and contributed the cases focusing on mathematics leadership issues. In 1987, the Exxon Education Foundation created what was to become one of its signature programs—the K–3 Mathematics Specialist Program. The K–3 program seeks to improve student learning in mathematics by strengthening teachers' grasp of both content and pedagogy. It is guided by the belief that change at the classroom level needs to be teacher-led and that a teacher-based mathematics specialist role can be an important resource for improving the way mathematics is taught in the primary grades. The emphasis on kindergarten through third grade reflects the belief that students' math-performance patterns are shaped in early school years, when the quality of mathematics instruction is traditionally weak. Over the course of the last twelve years, the Foundation has awarded approximately three hundred math specialists grants in over ninety-eight school districts throughout the United States.

The ideas and dilemmas portrayed in the cases on leadership in mathematics come from the findings of the K–3 Mathematics Specialist Program Evaluation, *Journeys in Change* (Moon and Hein 1995). Jean Moon, an associate professor at Lesley College in Cambridge, Massachusetts, and now Advisor to the ExxonMobil Foundation, authored a series of four cases from the *Journeys in Change* study. These cases were designed to capture the experiences, challenges, and issues common to many of the K–3 projects as they, and the mathematics specialist role, evolved over time. In so doing, they served as a dissemination tool for the *Journeys in Change* study. Since they were written, these cases have been used by a number of K–3 Mathematics Specialist projects as a way to reflect on their individual programs and develop an understanding of the complexities of leadership.

Education Development Center, Inc. (EDC), an international non-profit organization dedicated to promoting human development through education, was a key contributor in the compilation of this book. With 250 projects around the globe, EDC is one of the world's leading nonprofit education organizations. Founded in 1958, EDC conducts research and develops programs in such areas as early child development, K–12 education, health promotion, workforce preparation, learning technologies, and institutional reform. EDC specializes in creating and implementing training programs for teachers, health-care professionals, and other workers; designing curriculum materials dedicated to inquiry-based, hands-on learning; and conducting applied research on learning through the life span and in a wide variety of settings. EDC has a history of presenting research and framing issues in case form for education purposes. Recent work includes *Casebook on School Reform* (Miller and Kantrov 1998b) and *A Guide to Facilitating Cases in Education* (Miller and Kantrov 1998a).

Barbara Miller, Managing Project Director at EDC, worked with Susan Elko and Deborah Bryant Spencer in developing the MISE cases on mathematics teacher leadership, creating the facilitator's guides for those cases, and editing those materials for this volume. Miller also worked with Jean Moon to edit the Exxon cases and to create the facilitator's guides for those cases. She helped to field-test all the case materials and, as editor, worked to ensure that the book maintains connections to the experiences of real people who act as case facilitators. Miller was also the lead author of the introduction.

As with most books, this one took longer than any of us had anticipated. Our thanks go to Carlo Parravano, director of the Merck Institute for Science Education, to Ed Ahnert, president of the ExxonMobil Foundation, and to Robert Witte, recently retired senior program officer, for their consistent and enthusiastic support of this project. We appreciate the feedback received from those who field-tested the cases: Leader Teachers and principals in the four MISE Partnership districts; project directors, specialists, and teachers in the K–3 Mathematics Specialists programs; and colleagues at EDC who participated in case seminars. Elizabeth Badger deserves a special thank-you for her thoughtful reflections during the development of the ExxonMobil cases. Leigh Peake, editorial director at Heinemann, always thought that this book was a good idea, even when deadlines passed unmet, and we appreciate her consistent support. Many people at EDC also helped to make this book a reality, including Sarah Gray, Tony Artuso, Ilene Kantrov, Ellen Lubell, and Christine Farnsworth, and we thank them for their help and their ideas.

INTRODUCTION

Why a Casebook on Teacher Leadership?

A volume of cases might focus on any number of topics, and teacher leadership might be explored or developed through any number of means. Why, then, a casebook on teacher leadership? We have found case discussions to be a stimulating and engaging way to promote reflection, encourage problem solving, and build a shared set of ideas among a community of participants. Discussing one or more cases helps participants think about a compelling issue in context, in realistic settings with all their inherent complexity. Case discussions also help participants begin to tease an issue from its context, allowing them to explore its larger, theoretical implications or to consider how an issue plays out in other situations. Over the past few years, we have seen a greater use of cases in preservice and inservice settings and consequently, a greater interest in developing cases, facilitating and using cases, and understanding what kinds of learning are developed through case use. We see this volume as part of that growing interest.

Currently, the "case" idea is defined in different ways and used to reach different kinds of goals (Merseth 1996, Carter 1999). It is sometimes thought of as a snapshot of a real-life situation, preserved to exemplify particular practices, promote heated debate, resolve dilemmas, or document complicated changes (J. Shulman 1992, Sykes and Bird 1992). Others emphasize that the use of cases makes the "familiar strange and the simple complex" (Barnett 1998) by inviting users to consider a specific situation as representative of a larger class of issues or concerns (L. Shulman 1996). We like the dual images of a window and a mirror (see Miller and Kantrov 1998a): through cases, we can look into a particular situation and consider its features and issues in order to explore ideas and test out hypotheses while simultaneously comparing how the case experience helps us to reflect on our own experience.

The appeal of cases comes, in part, from their verisimilitude—they are realistic portrayals of some phenomenon. This realism is particularly appealing when it comes to teacher leadership. Teacher leaders may not be a new phenomenon in the field of education, but they certainly represent a new kind of role for the majority of teachers who act in this capacity. Access to realistic portrayals of teacher leadership affords a larger number of people the opportunity to see images of teacher leaders, to consider and resolve the kinds of problems they face, and to reflect on issues that impede or enhance their effectiveness. These case materials were developed for work with and by teacher leaders in science and mathematics and are collected here to support that development elsewhere.

The strength of the case materials in this volume contribute to both the analysis and the synthesis of ideas about teacher leadership. These cases are intended not as exemplars of teacher leadership but as narratives that illustrate themes common to teacher leadership work, the dilemmas that are often inherent in leadership, the roles that teacher leaders typically play, and the cast of characters that populate most leadership scenarios. They are designed to promote thoughtful reflection on teacher leadership by highlighting particular and possibly different leadership practices and to help teacher leaders and other educators consider the implications of teacher leadership in their own settings.

These case materials are imbued with a spirit of inquiry. Central to the facilitation materials and their structure are opportunities for participants to engage in questioning, hypothesizing, collecting data from their own experiences, using resources in the case text and facilitator's guide, and drawing and testing conclusions. We believe that the power of these cases comes from their use in discussion with others. Working with a group to consider different interpretations, alternative perspectives, and new approaches increases the opportunities for learning (Carter 1999, Levin 1999, Laframboise and Griffith 1997, J. Shulman 1996).

Why Use the Case Method?

There is a growing body of literature on the case method and its uses in education, and of research on its effectiveness (Lundeberg, Levin, and Harrington 1999, Colbert, Desberg, and Trimbel 1996, Merseth 1996, J. Shulman 1992). Although scholars may define cases differently and specify different purposes for cases and their use in discussion, there appears to be agreement about the storied nature of a case. A case is a story designed and presented to engage those using it to solve a problem, wrestle through a puzzle, discern an underlying principle, or stimulate reflection. Like other story formats, a case portrays character, emotion, setting, and dialogue (Kleinfeld 1996, Barnes, Hanson, and Christensen 1994, Barnett, Goldstein, and Jackson 1994).

The cases in this volume, like many of the others used in education, portray dilemmas that exist in complicated, multilayered situations. Because they are open-ended, they offer multiple pathways to explore. They present many well-rounded characters who approach the dilemmas from different perspectives, just as in real life. They contain sequenced events that add detail, heighten tension, and reflect the complexity of participants' own situations. Each of these cases was developed from actual leadership contexts. Some are slightly fictionalized accounts of actual events; some are composites based on dilemmas and characters drawn from several different situations. Regardless of their origin, they are all meant to promote thoughtful inquiry. They were designed for use in inservice and preservice settings to engage groups of participants and stimulate discussion and reflection.

These cases are rich and provocative, but we believe that their true power emerges when they are used in discussion by groups of participants, an enterprise that often calls for some degree of facilitation. Most available education cases include guidelines or suggestions for use with participants. These facilitation materials, whether they are a handful of suggested discussion questions or a set of extensive notes, enable participants to capitalize on the complex and multifaceted nature of the cases themselves. If one is seeking a "one answer fits all" scenario, this is not the place to look. Using cases in discussion usually requires some attention to the multiple perspectives portrayed in the cases themselves and represented by the participants discussing them. Engaging, probing discussion can extend over a period of hours or sessions, making cases good materials to use in intensive or ongoing professional development as advocated by educators calling for more serious and sustained learning by teachers (Loucks-Horsley et al. 1998, Little 1993).

Where Did These Cases Come From?

The cases in these volumes were developed under the auspices of particular teacher leadership programs. The Merck Institute for Science Education developed the case materials in Chapters 1, 2, and 3 as part of a leadership curriculum for their Leader Teachers Institute. Susan Elko field-tested each of the cases and facilitation materials with multiple groups of Leader Teachers who were working to promote science and mathematics reform in their districts. The cases in Chapters 4–7 were developed by Jean Moon for the ExxonMobil Foundation as part of the documentation of the K–3 Mathematics Specialist program. These specialists were teacher leaders engaged in mathematics reform in districts across the country. These cases were developed by and about real teacher leaders who were grappling with genuine issues and often new roles as they worked with classroom teachers, administrators, and parents to change elementary mathematics education.

The MISE and ExxonMobil cases have been brought together in this collection because together they provide an image of what teacher leadership in mathematics and science can look like in districts other than those for which the materials were first developed. The facilitation materials have been designed to emphasize teacher leadership themes and to provide clear guidance to facilitators who want to use the materials to investigate or develop teacher leadership work at their sites.

Why a Focus on Teacher Leadership?

The term *teacher leadership* is used widely among many different education reform efforts (Lord and Miller 2000, Weiss et al. 1999, Loucks-Horsley, Stiles, and Hewson 1996, Miller and Mark 1995, St. John et al. 1994). It generally refers to actions by teachers outside their own classrooms which involve an explicit or implicit responsibility to provide professional development to their colleagues, to influence their communities' or districts' policies, or to act as adjunct district staff to support changes in classroom practices among teachers. Defined in this way, teacher leadership obviously covers a broad terrain.

Some define teacher leadership simply as effecting change in others, a definition that captures an even wider array of activities (Loucks-Horsley et al. 1998, Moller and Katzenmeyer 1996, Lieberman, Saxl, and Miles 1988). According to this definition, many teachers would be considered teacher leaders if they were able to bring about some change in their colleagues through the power of hallway conversations, sharing resources, or providing a model for new practices. In very informal ways, teachers are leaders by virtue of their many individualized efforts to bring about change among their colleagues and communities.

It is important to look at teacher leadership carefully and critically, because so many reform efforts presume that teacher leaders, whether formally or informally, will help their colleagues change classroom practice. Leadership, like any other professional capacity, requires cultivation, practice, and reflection (Loucks-Horsley et al. 1998, Lambert 1998). We can develop that capacity through various uses of these case materials: exploring who teacher leaders are and the roles they play, considering the implications of subject matter for teacher leaders' work, investigating leadership themes that cut across cases, and focusing on the assorted individuals with whom teacher leaders interact. Each of these features is described below.

Roles

Teacher leaders go by different names: mentor teachers, specialists, resource teachers, lead teachers, and peer teachers. These names mean different things in different settings and refer to a broad array of actions. In this volume, we want to focus attention on those teacher leaders who hold a position or play a role that is identified by others as providing leadership for change. As these cases demonstrate, some teacher leaders have district-sanctioned, release-time roles (e.g., specialist) that involve an application process and delineated tasks. Others take on new leadership responsibilities, in addition to their teaching responsibilities, within an existing district program or a new initiative that presumes teachers will work with their colleagues to effect change (e.g., coach). These tacit leadership structures, often without a publicly identified role for teacher leaders, nonetheless place teachers in leadership positions relative to the rest of their colleagues. Still other teacher leaders are backed by their principal or by district staff to assume leadership roles within their building or district; they are appointed or recruited to fill particular leadership positions that meet local needs (e.g., committee chair). While the cases in this volume do not represent the entire range of roles teacher leaders play, they do focus on many of the responsibilities and issues teacher leaders face in K–8 settings.

Discussions of teacher leadership often start with the question: What do teacher leaders do? While we agree that it is important to understand the work that teacher leaders do, we also believe that a strictly functional approach underestimates the challenges of the teacher leader role. It is easy to reduce this role to a list of tasks. But this approach has real limitations, because the work that teacher leaders are called to do often doesn't translate into discrete tasks. Supporting change in classroom practice is a big charge. Although teacher leaders might do many different things to reach that goal, these actions don't usually conform neatly to items on a "to do" list.

We believe it a more effective strategy to approach teacher leadership as a mindset or a predilection that informs their actions. If we think about a leadership mindset, we start to imagine a broader set of capacities. For example, effective teacher leaders need specific skills to complete a particular task, such as designing a professional development workshop, but they also need a broader set of competencies, such as being able to elicit and integrate multiple perspectives or develop longer-term action plans. In considering the new and challenging work that teacher leaders might take on—such as building support among parents for science education reform or advocating professional development resources—it's important that we not reduce this work to discrete tasks. Effective teacher leadership usually demands a leadership perspective based on a set of beliefs about one's role or one's mission in effecting change in others. "Leadership" is more than the completion of a set of tasks or the fulfillment of the functions set out in a job description. We encourage users to explore teacher leadership issues in the cases and accompanying facilitator's guides as a way begin to develop this leadership mindset.

Subject Matter

This book offers teacher leadership cases in the two disciplines of mathematics and science. We see many similarities in the leadership roles within these contexts. Both mathematics and science education currently have reform agendas that are tied to national, state, and district standards. Both are linked to new curricula, instruction, and assessment. New materials in both disciplines call for a level of content knowledge often exceeding that possessed by many teachers of mathematics and science at all grade levels. Implementing mathematics and science education reform means large-scale changes for many classrooms and schools, during which teacher leaders are often at the forefront, working with colleagues, parents, and administrators.

At the same time, we acknowledge that there are important leadership differences between mathematics and science education reform. Mathematics tends to have a higher priority in most schools, particularly at the elementary level. The selection and widespread use of curricular materials also receives more attention in mathematics than in science, although in science there is less pressure over performance on high-stakes tests. These factors have implications for how teacher leadership work takes shape in each discipline. By considering these implications, we can develop a better understanding of the leadership challenges and opportunities in both areas of reform and benefit from the lessons learned in one discipline that apply to the other.

Leadership Themes

These teacher leadership cases offer a way to consider several critical themes often identified by teacher leaders in their work (see Figure I.1). Figure I.1 identifies the leadership themes in various cases to allow facilitators or case users to select those that address issues of particular interest. A particular theme, such as developing expertise, often emerges in more than one case, offering users an opportunity to explore that theme from several vantage points. This set of themes is not comprehensive, but it does represent the kinds of issues that teacher leaders encounter as they engage in leadership work in a school or districtwide context. As many teacher leaders have noted, acting in a leadership capacity is different from acting in a classroom teaching capacity, yet exactly what constitutes the work of teacher leaders and which issues teacher leaders should expect to face is not

Figure I.1: Teacher Leadership Themes

Teacher Leadership Theme	Chapter 1 Habitats	Chapter 2 Reaching Out	Chapter 3 Making the Case	Chapter 4 Specialist for All Seasons	Chapter 5 Who's the Expert Around Here?	Chapter 6 From Where I Stand	Chapter 7 Where Do We Go Next?
Developing expertise	✔	✔			✔		
Negotiating new relationships	✔			✔			
Dealing with resistant colleagues		✔			✔		
Building support among administrators			✔	✔		✔	
Securing resources and policy support						✔	✔
Developing a critical mass for change			✔				✔

always clear. Even with a clear job description and the experience of other teacher leaders to draw on, most teacher leaders find themselves trying to define, in relation to their previous role as classroom teacher, the functions that constitute teacher leadership at their site. We wish the question were as simple as "What is my job as a teacher leader?" Leadership issues represent many of the challenges that teacher leaders must resolve as they define the nature of their leadership.

To aid those using the Figure I.1 matrix in designing a case experience, we offer the following brief descriptions of these leadership themes and encourage readers to look more closely at the cases to see how these themes play out.

Developing Expertise

Many teacher leaders see themselves as leaders precisely because they have expertise to share, yet expertise can mean many different things. It can refer to their content knowledge within a discipline or in the particular curricula they draw on or impart to colleagues; to prior teaching experience across grade levels and with various student populations, which informs their actions; and to their skill in working with adults to promote their learning. Confusion arises when the kind of expertise needed by teacher leaders—or the expertise they are expected to develop in their colleagues—is not specified. Some teacher leaders are selected because of their preexisting expertise; others are expected to acquire expertise. In either situation, teacher leaders typically find themselves developing expertise at the same time they act to develop it in their colleagues.

Negotiating New Relationships

Acting as a teacher leader calls for new kinds of relationships with colleagues, principals, district staff, and community—relationships that are different from those in one's previous experience as a classroom teacher. Because teacher leaders need power and authority to effect change or to influence others, they struggle with questions about their own leadership authority and wonder whether they have the power they need to bring about change. In a profession viewed and experienced by a majority of teachers as egalitarian, with little differentiation in status even across long careers, teacher leaders mark out a new category, one that makes them different in some ways from their teaching peers. Leadership often involves renegotiating authority relationships as new demands arise or new players enter the picture.

Dealing with Resistant Colleagues

Resistance from teachers, administrators, and community members goes hand in hand with the change agendas that typically constitute the work of teacher leaders. Understanding resistance and learning how to deal with it in constructive rather than debilitating ways are important issues for teacher leaders, who can draw on their prior experience in confronting resistance from students over engaging in a particular activity or a specific discipline. However, the challenge of addressing resistance from peers raises questions about the interpersonal and strategic capacities of teacher leaders.

Building Support Among Administrators

While teacher leaders often conceive of their work as focused on teachers, they also know that it is critical to build wider networks of support for change efforts. This most often means administrators in a district or school, where principals and district staff need to be committed to the initiative. Without the support of those outside the classroom, teacher leaders are forced to rely primarily on the strength of their interactions with teachers and their persuasive power to engage classroom teachers in reform work.

Securing Resources and Policy Support

Teacher leadership is generally identified with the sharing of knowledge, ideas, or skills with classroom teachers. However, teachers are also effective leaders when they are able to provide needed resources, influence policies that affect classrooms, gather data about the need to change practice, and work to transform the larger culture in which particular teachers and classrooms function. The capacity of teacher leaders to access and influence these kinds of resources can ultimately determine whether new classroom practices succeed or fail.

Developing a Critical Mass for Change

In order for change to occur in systems as complex as schools, a sufficient number of like-minded colleagues need to share common goals and actions. While teacher leaders often work one-on-one with colleagues, they also need to address building a larger community of teachers committed to new practices. One aspect of the work of teacher leaders, therefore, is to figure out the "mathematics of change": What constitutes a critical mass of colleagues sufficient to sustain changes in practice? Another aspect is using various strategies to reach and sustain a group of teachers engaged in new classroom practices.

These teacher leadership themes take different forms. One theme—for example, negotiating new relationships—may be manifested when a teacher leader begins to develop a new working relationship with a former principal outside the classroom. This theme may also be present in those situations when a teacher leader takes on the role of instructor for a professional development workshop, particularly if this role involves asking other teachers to try strategies or consider ideas that are alien or uncomfortable. It is always useful to examine how a single theme plays out in different cases to develop a well-rounded understanding of its challenges and opportunities.

Clearly there is overlap among these themes. Negotiating new relationships is linked to dealing with resistance, since many teacher leaders may feel stymied in responding to resistance from colleagues because they lack the authority to tackle the very issues that make their colleagues resistant. Similarly, building support among principals and district staff is connected to developing a critical mass, since teacher leaders can often create momentum for change through their efforts to develop commitment and involvement among administrators. Because of this kind of overlap, it is useful to examine how related issues play out in different cases or to focus on one theme and use it as the springboard for considering other related themes.

Leadership Case Characters

We offer another way to think about teacher leadership, by focusing on the characters or individuals involved in teacher leadership work. The presence or absence of certain characters in the teacher leadership scenarios in these cases conveys information about what is meant by leadership by teachers. Figure I.2 (see p. 10) shows the characters featured in various cases, so that facilitators or case users may select cases that focus on characters of particular interest.

To aid in using the matrix in designing a case experience, we offer the following brief descriptions of these categories and encourage readers to look more closely at the cases to see them "in action."

Individual teacher leaders may be released from the classroom or they may be full-time classroom teachers with additional leadership

Figure I.2: Teacher Leadership Case Characters

Teacher Leadership Theme	Chapter 1 Habitats	Chapter 2 Reaching Out	Chapter 3 Making the Case	Chapter 4 Specialist for All Seasons	Chapter 5 Who's the Expert Around Here?	Chapter 6 From Where I Stand	Chapter 7 Where Do We Go Next?
Teacher leader (individual)	✔		✔	✔	✔	✔	✔
Teacher leaders (group)		✔			✔		✔
Classroom teacher(s)	✔	✔	✔		✔		✔
Principal	✔	✔	✔	✔		✔	✔
District staff				✔	✔		✔
Community members			✔				✔

responsibilities. In cases featuring individual teacher leaders, the emphasis is on the challenges and opportunities a specific teacher leader faces. *Groups of teacher leaders* can work together, each one acting as a support to the others, or as a team in which different members take on different roles. In cases featuring groups of teacher leaders, the focus is on what a particular group of leaders might learn from one another or achieve with the help of one another.

Classroom teachers are the typical audience for or recipients of teacher leadership. At the same time, many teacher leaders identify themselves most strongly as classroom teachers, raising questions about the distinction between teacher and leader. In cases featuring classroom teachers, much of the action centers on teacher leaders' interactions with their colleagues in the classroom. *Principals* are the traditional leader figures within a school, and yet teacher leaders are often called upon to interact with or act in concert with building principals. At least some of the emphasis in the cases featuring principals is on the teacher leader/principal relationship.

District staff refers to a district's central office staff, including superintendents and assistant superintendents, subject area specialists, and other midlevel managers within a school system. In cases featuring district staff, the focus is on the role they play in promoting or hindering teacher leader effectiveness. *Community members*, depending on the particular case, may include parents of students, members of the business community, or university faculty. In cases featuring community members, the focus is on the issues and concerns these individuals bring to the table for teacher leaders to address in some way.

How Are the Case Materials Structured?

This volume contains seven chapters, each consisting of the case text and a facilitator's guide. These components underscore the importance we place on active and purposeful facilitation of these cases, ideas we discuss in greater detail later. In the discussion that follows the case text, we are speaking to you in the role of case facilitator. We use the term "participants" to refer to those individuals who take part in reading, discussing, and using the case according to the plan you have developed.

Cases

The seven cases in this book present situations in which teacher leaders are central players. By reading and working with the text of each case, participants develop an understanding of the particular constellation of dilemmas the teacher leader(s) in that case face as well as the issues they confront. In the three cases developed in the MISE project, the teacher leaders assume the roles of coach, instructor, or advocate. In the four cases that came from the ExxonMobil project, the mathematics specialist(s) play a variety of leadership roles.

The selection of a case depends on the purpose of a case discussion. Most often, facilitators or users select a case because "it's just like us." It's important to select a story line like your own, but we would advise you not to shy away from cases about mathematics teacher leaders "because we're science" or those featuring teacher leaders who are full-time classroom teachers "because we have teacher leaders who are out of the classroom full-time." Pay more attention to the issues addressed by particular cases and construct a case experience that helps participants consider those issues. Look for a case that offers more than a surface match. Through discussion, reflection, and work, case participants develop an understanding of the specific teacher leadership issues involved. Simply reading a case with a similar story line will not develop knowledge about—or skills in—teacher leadership. These cases are not meant to be neat. Rather, they are complex and unresolved, features that point to the importance of your facilitation.

The length of these cases is such that each can be read in ten to fifteen minutes. This reading time might be followed by group discussion and activities. Or the reading might take place before the group comes together for discussion. Since these cases do not have study questions at the end you may want to add them, using the facilitator's guide for ideas. In addition, reading is generally more productive when participants mark passages of interest, note evidence to back up their opinions or inferences, indicate actions or exchanges they find confusing or compelling, or scribble comments in the margins. This record of participant's reflections is often useful during the various activities described in the facilitation materials.

Stance Toward Facilitation

We see the role of facilitator as central to the productive and thoughtful use of these cases. It need not be a formally assigned role or a predetermined set of actions. We think that the act of facilitating— articulating purpose, selecting activities, moderating discussion, drawing out conclusions—contributes to greater insights on the part of participants. In earlier work, Miller has referred to the facilitator as the one who helps to create a case experience by using the case and the facilitation materials to raise the level of inquiry and promote deeper understanding (Miller and Kantrov 1998a, 1998b). During a case experience, more than one person might share facilitation responsibilities, or developing the capacity of the group to share facilitation might be a goal. The point is that facilitation is important to the case experience, and we have designed the facilitation materials with this assumption in mind.

In preparing these materials, we have tried to provide helpful but not overwhelming suggestions. A critical point, which we address consistently throughout, is the importance of clarifying the purpose of using a particular case. Each case includes more than one leadership theme, and we know from past experience that facilitators and participants often focus on other issues they find salient. Beyond the presence of different themes, we also know that there is no one "typical" case discussion and that the discussion changes depending on the particular group of participants and their interests as well as their level of experience with casework. This means that as facilitator, you need to be as clear as you can about the intended purpose of using a particular case with a particular group of participants.

Facilitation is most successful when there is a balance between what the case offers as a compelling leadership narrative, what the case facilitator wants to address in the discussion, and what the participants in the case experience are seeking (see Figure I.3). This interplay between case, facilitator, and participant is not unique to casework; similar manifestations are seen in analyses of curriculum (see Hawkins 1974). However, this image of triangulation underscores the fact that case facilitation is an important activity that occurs in response to participants' interests and knowledge and in relation to the case's potential to raise important questions. The case experience represents the interaction of these three features. For a longer discussion on case facilitation, along with suggestions for structuring a productive agenda and working effectively with groups, we encourage you to examine *A Guide to Facilitating Cases in Education* (Miller and Kantrov 1998a).

Figure I.3: **Constructing a Case Experience**

Features of Case Facilitation Materials

The facilitator's guide following each case includes a case summary, a list of the leadership issues addressed, a sequenced set of activities for guiding discussion, and sidebar notes with tips and additional resources. Each is further described below. These materials are meant to offer structure without dictating action. Thus, we have tried to be explicit about why we recommend certain actions or outline particular questions so that you can apply your judgment in using or adapting the materials.

Case Summary

The case summary at the beginning of each facilitator's guide contains a brief overview of the action of the case to identify the major characters. You can use this summary to refresh your memory about the scenario portrayed in the case, but we would caution you not to substitute the summary for the case text itself. It is important that participants read and consider carefully the story line that unfolds in the case rather than rely on the condensed version in the synopsis.

Leadership Themes

Following each case summary is a list of the two teacher leadership issues the case addresses (see Figure I.1, p. 7). Although most of these cases touch on other leadership issues as well, we indicate the two we think are most clearly portrayed. Reviewing the teacher leadership issues can help you articulate the purpose of the case experience, guide you in selecting particular activities, and help you to focus the attention of participants during the case discussion.

Summary of Activities

Each facilitator's guide includes six or seven sets of activities. Each activity set consists of up to seven different activities that you might choose to do with participants: small-group discussions around particular questions, large-group discussions, individual reflection prompts, role plays, etc. For each set, we have indicated the format used and the estimated time needed to do all the individual activities.

In sequencing the sets of activities, we have employed a framework that utilizes the case in three different ways: working within the case, expanding upon the case, and moving beyond the case (Miller and Kantrov 1998b). Each facilitator's guide outlines two sets of activities that work within the case, in which participants are asked to focus on the story and the characters' actions in order to become familiar with the text so they can use it as a common point of reference in discussion. Participants are then ready for activities that expand upon the case. In these activities, participants engage in more interpretive work, drawing upon prior experiences, ideas developed in discussion, and inferences from the case text. At this point, participants can more easily move beyond the case to consider the issues that carry over to their own situation or to analyze a theme that goes beyond the story line or the concerns raised in the case.

In structuring a case experience, we encourage you to follow this sequence—working within, expanding upon, and moving beyond the case—even if you choose to do only a few of the activities in the facilitator's guide. (See Figure I.4 for an example based on the facilitator's guide in Chapter 4, "Specialist for All Seasons," that plays out two different case experiences.)

This sequence conveys some important benefits. First, *working within the case* establishes a shared understanding of the case text. It also allows you to elicit or identify issues that will be pursued further in the discussion. Grounded in the case text, the opening sets of activities are structured to involve all participants in the discussion, an important dynamic to establish at the outset. Moreover, working within

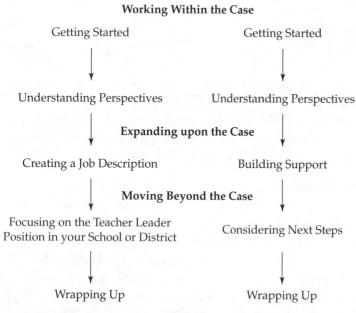

Figure I.4: Sequence of Activities
Specialist for All Seasons

the case, where the dilemma is paramount and no resolution is presented, slows the headlong rush to simplistic problem solving. Many participants approach cases as dilemmas to be resolved and, although this is a useful purpose for a case experience, problem solving will be richer and more thought provoking if participants engage in this kind of preliminary work.

The facilitator's guides also present many sets of activities for *expanding upon the case*. These activities support investigation of the leadership themes, develop skills, or build on ideas presented in the case itself. They draw on insights from the initial activities but begin to elaborate on the story line. Problem solving goes on in some of these activities, but it is grounded in the exploration of a wider set of ideas than those individual participants may have brought to the case experience.

Finally, toward the end of the case experience, we offer sets of activities for *moving beyond the case* so that participants can utilize the ideas developed in earlier activities and discussions. A range of problem-solving opportunities is outlined, from imagining the next steps in the case to anticipating outcomes in several different scenarios. In addition, we also offer activities that ask participants to apply ideas from the case experience to their own situations.

Each chapter includes three common sets of activities: "Getting Started," "Understanding Perspectives," and "Wrapping Up," and we recommend doing at least one activity from each of these sets. It is important to work within the case, and "Getting Started" activities are the easiest way to do so, because they help participants talk about the features of the case, identify the major issues, describe the characters, and articulate the story line. On a basic level, they ensure that the participants are all working with the same set of facts and envisioning the same flow of events. They are also a useful way to state the range of issues, setting the stage for you to choose or negotiate the issues that will frame the entire case experience.

In all seven chapters, we outline a variety of "Getting Started" activities. The Strategies Index (see Appendix A, p. 139) lists the various "Getting Started" activities, each designed to engage, at the outset, the greatest number of participants. This sets a collaborative tone for the case experience and creates an opportunity for you, as facilitator, to discuss any expectations about participation in the discussion. Inclusive activities such as those found in "Getting Started" underscore the importance of full involvement by all participants.

The "Understanding Perspectives" activities are powerful ways to engage participants in the characters' concerns and motivations, which often become a platform from which they can compare or contrast their own ideas. "Understanding Perspectives" consists of discussion questions, exercises, and reflections that focus on the opinions and ideas held by various characters. Through these activities, participants become more grounded in the case as they develop a greater familiarity with the characters' intentions and actions. They can also begin to use evidence from the case to fashion an interpretation of the characters' thoughts, motives, and experiences.

Finally, the "Wrapping Up" activities help participants to bring some closure to the case experience. You should adapt these activities, or substitute some from another chapter, to fit the goals of the case experience (see Appendix A, Strategies Index).

Specific Activities

Each set of activities in the facilitator's guides consists of two to seven specific activities: small- and large-group discussions, individual reflection, role plays, pair and triad activities, and debates. We don't assume that you will necessarily use all the individual activities. In fact, the discussions will be more productive if participants do a small number of activities in their entirety rather than abbreviated versions of a larger number. We have outlined each activity in sufficient detail to allow an informed choice among them. The selections you make should reflect the purpose of the case experience. The time estimates came from field tests of the case materials and are presented as a range of possible times. We encourage you to try out each activity prior to doing the activity with participants. This is particularly important for discussion activities, since this is an opportunity to consider what responses might be offered and in what directions the conversation might move.

Sidebar Text

The facilitator's guides all have a similar layout. Comments addressed directly to you, as the facilitator, are located in the inside column of each page to form a kind of running commentary on the activities or ideas presented in the guide. In many instances, these notes grew out of field-test experiences within the case materials and include tips on facilitating the group and managing discussion as well as on facilitating the case through particular choices or adaptations of activities. For an elaboration of facilitation strategies, see Miller and Kantrov (1998b).

In the sidebar text we have tried to be more explicit about some of the assumptions that go into case facilitation. There are references to educational literature that explores the leadership themes featured in a case experience as well as additional resources. In some places, we offer further explanations of an activity; in others, we provide more background information. The sidebar text also includes suggestions for extending activities, either during or outside the case discussion.

For the most part, the sidebar text is specific to each chapter, with one exception. One of the initial sidebars cautions against moving too quickly into problem solving, which seems to be the natural tendency in case discussions. The facilitator's guides include many pages of activities and discussion questions all meant to reinforce the idea that a case experience is intended to achieve more than simply answering the query "What should Gina (or Leo or Beth or Roger) do next?" The sidebars offer additional ideas.

Strategies Index

In the Strategies Index (Appendix A) we have highlighted strategies of special interest to you, as the facilitator, and noted the page numbers of other examples of the same kind of activities, such as, "Getting Started," in each of the six chapters. Variations on the same activity can help you tailor the case experience to the strengths of particular participants.

How Might the Cases Be Used?

We anticipate that these case materials will be used in various contexts: in teacher inservice as part of a program to support or develop teacher leaders—for example, a two-hour after-school workshop, an ongoing seminar series, or as the curriculum for a study group—and in preservice courses at the graduate or undergraduate level in combination with other resources addressing teacher leadership in school reform. We offer suggestions on how the case materials might be used singly or in combination, and used once or multiple times. Again, their use is determined by the purpose of the case experience.

Here is an example. Let's assume that you are putting together resources for a group of science teachers preparing to take on leadership responsibility in their schools. You might begin by identifying the leadership themes you would like teachers to examine together and choose cases accordingly (see Figure I.1). For example, you might want participants to focus initially on issues of developing expertise and renegotiating relationships with fellow teachers. For this purpose, you might select "Habitats" and "Who's the Expert Around Here?" These two cases allow participants to compare case situations and distinguish expertise issues in the case story, a useful investigation as they start their own work as teacher leaders. Then, to address negotiating new relationships, you might select "Specialist for All Seasons" for discussion, followed by a return to "Habitats" and the theme of negotiating new relationships. In this way, you could take advantage of participants' familiarity with the story and characters in "Habitats" to consider a different theme.

Take this example a bit further. The next step in this teacher leadership program might involve articulating productive ways for a group of teacher leaders to work together. To this end, you might select "Reaching Out," which looks at such a group, and then return to, "Who's the Expert Around Here?" Here, the *characters* presented in the case (see Figure I.2, p. 10) drive your selection of cases. You might also want to do some skill development and choose additional cases accordingly, returning to "Habitats" a third time to develop and practice communication skills or rehearse how teacher leaders might approach and engage their fellow teachers about classroom practice issues.

Our point is that cases can be used in various ways. They can be paired to explore how the same theme unfolds in different situations or how certain characters interact in new situations. They can be "repurposed" and reused, with a new focus. Sequences of cases can be put together in an overall case curriculum. These materials, in other words, are flexible, and, in the facilitator's guide we have tried to provide sufficient detail for "mixing and matching" as needed.

We encourage you to be creative in using these case materials. We have identified the range of leadership issues and the characters in each case to make it easy for you to locate the cases that address the issues important in your work. The Strategies Index makes it possible to use an activity outlined in one chapter with a case in another chapter. These approaches underscore our belief that evocative and effective cases are much more than stories that mimic participants' own situations. They are texts that can sustain thoughtful inquiry into important issues. They provide a window into new situations, with dilemmas and settings that may be quite different from those experienced by participants, and hold up a mirror that allows them to consider the implications for their own work.

CHAPTER 1

Habitats

Case

Gina Caruso, Third-grade teacher, Jefferson Elementary School
Pat Brown, Third-grade teacher
Maureen Hart, Principal

"Okay, what's next?" Jake asked. "We've put the black paper in, and it covers all four walls. What do we do next? Check the sheet." Jake jumped up from his chair and looked over the shoulder of his partner, Aaron, at the worksheet Aaron was holding.

"Lemme see . . . okay, that was step number four," said Aaron. "Now, step number five is 'Take the container of soil and spread it on the bottom of the terrarium.'"

"Ms. Caruso, where's the soil?" Jake asked. Gina Caruso was walking around the room, watching the pairs of third graders construct their terrariums. "Did you check the materials table?" she replied.

"Okay, let's get the soil from the materials table," said Jake, and the two boys hurried over to the side of the classroom, where a large table held buckets of soil, small plants, and other terrarium makings. Pat Brown was at the table, helping pairs of children to locate the materials they needed.

Gina and Pat were both third-grade teachers at Jefferson Elementary School. Gina had been teaching inquiry-based science for a couple of years, using science units or kits designed for hands-on exploration. Jefferson had recently decided to use the kits throughout the school, from kindergarten through sixth grade, and Gina was thrilled with the decision. She'd been teaching with kits for most of the last few years.

But for many teachers at Jefferson, it meant a big change from the textbook-based science curriculum they had been using.

Pat, Gina's grade-level teaching partner, had never taught using an inquiry-based approach before, and she had never used a kit either. On their inservice days the previous summer, Gina had worked with Pat to help her get oriented to teaching with a kit. She had had a brainstorm and shared it with Pat: What if they brought their classes together for science while Pat was getting used to the kits? Pat had agreed to try it. Gina had taught the first unit of the year to their combined classes, a kit on plant growth and development, and Pat had assisted her and observed. Now Pat was teaching the next unit, on habitats, and Gina was the one assisting and observing. They brought their classes together for science for two-hour blocks of time on Tuesdays and Thursdays.

Pat was about two weeks into the unit on habitats. During the first week, the students had explored their school as a habitat. In the second week, pairs of students had identified a microhabitat on the school grounds and had spent an extended period of time exploring their habitat and making observations about it.

Now, on the first Tuesday of the third week, Pat was having the students work in pairs to make terrariums. The students had brought insects and other small animals in from the school grounds and were creating terrariums to house the organisms. Pat had constructed a worksheet for the lesson from which the students were working.

Gina walked over to another pair of students, Tasha and Chris. They were placing insects into their terrariums. "Hold the bug box still," cried Tasha. "I've almost got him!" She held a cotton swab into the bug box and waited for an earthworm to crawl onto it. "Here's your new house, wormy!" she exclaimed as she transferred the worm from the bug box to the terrarium.

From what Gina could observe, Tasha and Chris, like Jake and Aaron, were engaged and having fun in the activity. But she didn't hear them talking about the terrariums as habitats or about what the organisms would need to survive—the critical elements of the lesson. The terrarium was an important part of the habitats unit because in designing a terrarium, children had to make decisions about what constitutes the important features of a habitat and how the terrarium can support the earthworms, slugs, and small creatures that live in it. In designing their terrariums, the students would have to work from their own observations of the school and the school yard as habitats, and implement their understanding of the important elements of habitats.

"That worksheet," Gina thought to herself, "takes all the science right out of this lesson. It's hands-on, all right, but not really inquiry-based science."

"In fact," she ruminated as she wandered about the room, helping students spread the soil in the terrariums and place the creatures and plants, "it's not even really science. It's just putting the pieces of the terrarium together. Pat's done the science for them." By telling children what the elements of the terrarium should be, and providing step-by-step instructions for preparing it, Pat had, unwittingly, taken the science out of the lesson.

Gina had been concerned about the unit from the beginning. Pat was doing well in terms of getting the students engaged and getting the activities organized and flowing, but there was something missing. The explorations the students had done of the habitats on the playground were interesting and, again, Pat had had all the students engaged. But Gina hadn't seen Pat make use of those observations when they talked about the terrariums or started putting them together. It was as if the habitat observations and the terrarium activity were not linked.

Pat paused near Gina on her way to help another pair of children place their creatures in the terrariums. She put her hand on Gina's shoulder and said, "It's going pretty well, huh? I think we might even be able to finish up somewhere near on time today!"

"You're right," laughed Gina. "That's always a challenge when you're doing hands-on anything. Are we going to sit down for a few minutes after school today and go over our plans for the rest of the week?"

"Sure," agreed Pat. "Why don't we meet down here in my classroom? All the stuff is here anyway. At three o'clock?"

Gina nodded. As Pat walked to the other side of the room, Gina wondered what she could say to Pat this afternoon to make her realize that this just wasn't working as well as it could. "Or," she thought, "maybe I shouldn't say anything at all to Pat right now. After all, she needs my support and encouragement. It took her a long time even to try this approach."

■ ■ ■

Gina was on her hands and knees in the science equipment closet, looking through boxes. "How's it going?" asked Maureen Hart, the principal at Jefferson Elementary, as she poked her head in the doorway. "Got a new project going?"

"Well, you could say that," Gina said. "I'm just trying to pull some things together for Pat. She's teaching habitats with our classes right now, and I'm helping and observing." She stood up and brushed the dust off her skirt.

"How's the observing going?" Maureen asked.

Gina furrowed her brow. "Well, it's going okay. Pat's really trying hard."

Maureen paused. "Sounds like something might be going wrong?"

"No, not wrong. Just hard. I mean, I see her do things that I did when I first started this inquiry-based science teaching, and I remember how hard it was. And I think, who am I to tell to her what to do? It's not as if I'm a real expert at this. It's not as if I'm the master of scientific inquiry!" Gina looked at Maureen quickly and swallowed nervously. She thought to herself, did I say too much?

Maureen looked concerned. "Gina, don't worry about it. You do know what you're doing. You've had a lot of training and support for science. You're our science person. You know more about it than almost anyone else on the faculty."

"But Maureen, that's just it. I mean, everyone keeps thinking I'm the science person, and I don't know that I'm always doing the right thing. I mean, I wouldn't hold myself up as exemplary."

"Look, Gina, I have complete confidence in you. You are doing the right thing. You keep up the good work and it'll all work itself out." Maureen gave her shoulder a friendly pat and turned and walked down the hallway.

■ ■ ■

Gina walked into Pat's room at three o'clock, after the children had gone home. Pat was rearranging supplies in the science area. She looked up, saw Gina, and said, "Hi there. So, what did you think about today?"

Gina joined her in straightening out the supplies. "I thought it was pretty good. You seemed very comfortable with the lesson, and the kids were definitely engaged." She paused, "The worksheet is new. What made you decide to use that?"

"Well," said Pat, "I wanted to be sure that all the kids were able to make the terrarium, and I didn't want them to make it wrong. Otherwise they would have had to start all over again. And it was very confusing for them with all those parts. So, last night, when I was going over the lesson, I put together the diagrams and the steps to keep it organized."

"Do you think they might have explored a little bit more if they hadn't had the worksheet?" asked Gina casually.

"Well, they might have, but I don't think they would have been able to finish the terrarium. It probably would have taken all week, and we would be behind schedule." Pat stopped what she was doing, looked at Gina quizzically and asked, "Why, do you think I didn't do it right? I put a lot of time into that lesson today."

"No, no, it's not that," Gina reassured Pat quickly. "The effort you put in really showed, it did. I guess I was just checking to see if you were feeling good about the exploration the kids were doing."

"Actually, you know, it was kind of exciting," Pat smiled, looking relieved. "The kids really seemed to have fun with the terrariums, actually whenever we're working hands-on with the materials. I think Jake and Aaron were really excited when they finally got the terrarium together right. And the kids did a lot of neat things with the habitats during the explorations last week."

Gina hesitated, unsure what to say. On the one hand, Pat seemed very enthusiastic about the class and about the children's excitement, and she didn't want to discourage her. On the other hand, Gina felt that Pat, in the approach she was taking, was missing some important opportunities for the children to be learning about habitats.

"Well, yeah, I think you're right. The explorations last week were nice. The children were exploring, finding the insects, and investigating their environments. Maybe we could think about how to remind them about that experimentation when they're thinking about refining their terrariums," Gina suggested.

"Okay, I can try to do that. I think I'll put together a set of questions in a worksheet for Thursday's lesson. And I'll include one that refers to the experimentation," Pat offered. She went to her desk, opened her planner, and began to make a note of it.

"Pat," Gina said, with some trepidation, "maybe the students don't need a worksheet. Maybe they could figure some of the steps out themselves."

Pat paused and looked intently at Gina. "What are you trying to say, Gina? I don't get where you're coming from. On the one hand, you say I'm doing fine, but on the other, it sounds as if you don't think it's going so well. What do you really think about how the unit is working?"

Gina hesitated, unsure of what to say. She wondered, "What do I really think? And what can I say to Pat?"

Facilitator's Guide

Summary of the Case

Gina Caruso and Pat Brown, two third-grade teachers at Jefferson Elementary School, have teamed up to teach a hands-on, inquiry-based science unit on habitats. Pat is new to teaching this unit and new to this type of teaching, while Gina has used similar units in her classroom for the past couple of years. Gina and Pat worked together on a previous unit, Gina teaching, and Pat assisting and observing. With the habitats unit, their roles are reversed.

As the case opens, Gina is observing Pat teach a lesson in which the children are building terrariums. Although the children are engaged, the lesson raises concerns for Gina. She feels that Pat has overdirected the lesson, providing children with information about what should be in a terrarium rather than engaging them in thinking about the science of the lesson, namely, the elements of a habitat that will allow living creatures to survive.

In the second scene, we see Gina in a brief interaction with Jefferson's principal, Maureen Hart. Gina expresses to Maureen her concerns about whether she has the expertise to be guiding Pat. Maureen offers Gina reassurances about her expertise and expresses her confidence in Gina.

In the final scene, Gina and Pat meet after school to talk. Gina makes indirect suggestions to Pat about improvements in that day's lesson and in subsequent lessons. Pat presses Gina to tell her how the unit is going. Gina is unsure how to respond: on the one hand, she feels that Pat needs to make several improvements in her teaching of the unit; on the other hand, she does not want to discourage Pat.

Leadership Themes

This case focuses on a particular teacher leader role, that of classroom coach, and raises questions about the relationship between a teacher leader and other teachers in the building. Gina, the coach, wonders about the nature of her expertise and the ways in which that expertise shapes her interactions with colleagues and with her principal.

This case provides an opportunity for discussion around

- *Negotiating new relationships:* How does a teacher leader establish collegial relationships with other teachers, especially in a climate of isolation? How does a teacher leader act as a leader while still in many ways remaining in the more egalitarian position of a teacher among other teachers?
- *Developing expertise:* To what extent does a teacher leader share his or her own knowledge and extensive expertise or insist that others discover ideas for themselves? What is the balance between the two approaches?

Summary of Activities

This guide offers six sets of suggested activities designed to support discussion of the case. You should feel free to add or delete activities, adapt them to suit your purposes, or reorder the activities to fit the needs of the group with which you will be working. As presented here, the sets of activities are structured to focus first on the content of the case itself and then to consider larger issues beyond the immediate case scenario related to the leadership themes. Estimates of the total amount of time needed, if one were to do all the activities in a set, are given in parentheses. Time estimates for individual activities are given in the descriptions that follow.

The six sets of activities are as follows:

- *Getting Started:* A large-group discussion of alternative case titles designed to aid consideration of the range and variety of the issues in the case (20–30 minutes)
- *Understanding Perspectives:* A sequence of small- and large-group activities designed to focus discussion on understanding and analyzing different perspectives on a coaching relationship between two colleagues (90–125 minutes)
- *Exploring the Coaching Relationship:* An individual written reflection followed by small- and large-group discussion to articulate different kinds of coaching experiences (45–65 minutes)
- *Communicating Feedback:* Small- and large-group activities designed to look at the quality of the communication between Gina and Pat, specifically in the final scene (80–120 minutes)
- *Considering Ground Rules:* A paired role-play activity in which participants step away from the story line of the case and take on the roles of Pat and Gina in order to consider the ground rules for a successful coaching relationship (55–75 minutes)
- *Wrapping Up:* An individual written reflection followed by a large-group discussion to identify ideas about coaching to take away from the discussion (15–25 minutes)

Getting Started

This initial discussion activity is intended to support participants in developing a common understanding of the range and variety of issues in the case and to encourage participants to articulate problems and issues.

Large-group discussion (20–30 minutes)

Distribute an index card to each participant and ask that each person write a new title for the case using as few words as possible. Suggest beginning with "The Case of . . . ," in the spirit of the late 1950s television show, *Perry Mason*.

After participants have had time to write a title on the index card, ask them to pass the index cards around their table (or other natural

Some facilitators have been known to hum the dramatic theme song to the old Perry Mason TV show to reinforce this idea. This part of this activity is for participants to be economical in their titles. Completing the phrase "The Case of . . ." means creating a title that would fit on a book cover or fill the space of a television screen and no more.

grouping). Collect the pack of index cards from one table and pass it along to another table, continuing in this way until all participants have read each other's index cards. Ask each participant to jot brief notes as they read the index cards so they remember the titles they think are most appropriate as well as any titles about which they have questions or would like discussion. After the index cards have been passed around, begin the large-group discussion with questions such as

- Which title did you think best captured the essence of this case? Why?
- Did any of these titles share a particular focus?
- What questions did you have about a particular title, especially if you thought it was intriguing but weren't quite sure of its meaning?

In the course of discussing titles, try to listen for any confusion about the story line and the details of the case. Ask participants to clarify points in the case using evidence from the case to illustrate their thinking. Suggest that they refer to a particular page and paragraph when they cite their evidence. This sends participants back to the case text and offers useful clarification at this early stage.

Understanding Perspectives

Each of the adult characters in the case (Gina, Pat, and Maureen) has a perspective, a set of beliefs or a mindset about coaching relationships between professional colleagues, about what it means to be a coach and what it means to be coached. Likewise, participants in the case discussion will also have a set of beliefs or a mindset about Gina and Pat's coaching relationship as well as about coaching relationships in general. The following set of activities focuses first on understanding the perspectives represented by the characters in the case and then moves away from the story line by asking participants to reflect on their own experiences and beliefs related to coaching relationships in professional settings.

Small-group discussion (20–30 minutes)

The case provides the most data on Gina's view of coaching as she struggles to define her coaching relationship with Pat. Ask participants to work in groups of three or four to identify Gina's concerns and beliefs. Helpful discussion questions include

- How would Gina explain her coaching role to another teacher? Cite the evidence from the case on which you base your answer.
- What adjectives would *you* use to describe Gina's approach to her role as coach to Pat?
- What seems to be most challenging about the coaching role for Gina?

In discussing titles, listen for those that are popular with many people or ask for a show of hands ("How many of you made a note of this title?").

If the group consists of fewer than fifteen people, you might use a variation of the index card activity in which participants print their titles on 3 × 5 Post-it notes using markers to make them easy to read. Post these on a piece of newsprint in a designated area for everyone to read and consider. While people gather to read the Post-its, you can begin discussing categories, physically moving Post-its to reflect these categories.

A natural temptation for participants during this first large-group discussion is to want to offer solutions to the compelling dilemma at the end of the case. The challenge for you as the facilitator is to keep participants on track identifying the issues represented in the case (i.e., defining the problem). Here, it is more important to identify the range of issues participants see in the case than to move into solving one particular problem.

Prepare worksheets with these questions and have participants individually reflect and write their responses before they engage in discussion in their small groups.

Large-group discussion (15–20 minutes)

Have spokespersons from each small group contribute to a discussion of the same questions by the whole group. Record contributions on an overhead transparency or on newsprint. As facilitator, you may want to offer a synthesis of trends you see in the group's interpretations.

During this discussion you are listening for and prompting conversation around ideas related to the two leadership themes: negotiating new relationships and developing expertise. At this stage, it is sufficient to be noting and naming those points in the discussion that speak to new relationships or to expertise. These themes will be developed in later activities.

Small-group discussion (15–20 minutes)

In contrast to Gina's explicit perspective on the coaching relationship in the case text, much of Pat's perspective is implicit. Ask participants to work on the following questions in small groups:

- What does Pat believe Gina's role as her coach to be? What evidence illustrates these beliefs?
- What adjectives would you use to describe Pat's view of being coached by Gina?
- What are Pat's concerns about the coaching relationship?

Ask participants to write down the adjectives they would use to describe Pat's view of being coached by Gina on large Post-it notes using markers or thick pens so that the words are visible. Place the Post-it notes on newsprint to create a group list.

Large-group discussion (15–20 minutes)

In the larger group, ask participants to move the Post-it notes around on the newsprint to create clusters of similar adjectives and to label these clusters as a way to summarize the adjectives. Use these labels in the large-group discussion of Pat's perspective on Gina's role as a coach and her view of being coached by Gina.

Small-group discussion (15–20 minutes)

In the case text, Maureen's perspective on coaching is represented in two ways: through her view of Gina's coaching of Pat and through her own coaching of Gina. Ask participants, again working in small groups, to consider Maureen's perspective.

- Put yourself in Maureen's place and look at the coaching relationship between Gina and Pat. What are Maureen's beliefs about the coaching relationship? What evidence of those beliefs do you find in the text?

- Now put yourself in Maureen's place in working with Gina. Do you think Maureen is a coach to Gina? If so, what adjectives would you use to describe her approach to coaching Gina?

Large-group discussion (10–15 minutes)

Ask small groups to share their analysis. Begin with Maureen's views of Gina's coaching and then move on to Maureen's views of herself as a coach. In the large group, explore how these views on coaching (Gina as coach of Pat and Maureen as coach of Gina) are similar and different. Extend the discussion by asking the large group to consider this question:

- How could Maureen best support Gina in coaching Pat?

Exploring the Coaching Relationship

Understanding the perspectives of Gina, Pat, and Maureen can help participants reflect on their expectations of themselves (or others) as coaches. The following activities are designed to help participants produce clearly articulated examples of ways in which teachers can coach one another.

Individual written reflection (10–15 minutes)

Begin by alerting participants that you are now switching the focus of the discussion to their own beliefs about coaching, with the intended goal of articulating examples of teachers coaching one another. Drawing on the earlier discussions of the characters' perspectives, ask participants to consider at least one of the first three questions below in individual reflective writing and then respond to the final question:

- In this situation, imagine that you are Gina. What would you be thinking or feeling about your coaching relationship with Pat? What would your intention or goal be in coaching Pat?
- Has a colleague ever coached you? What did that colleague say to you? What was his or her intention? How did that feel to you? How would you describe your relationship with that colleague?
- Reflect on an experience in which you acted as a coach or imagine a situation in which you could possibly be a coach. Describe that situation. What did (would) you do as a coach?
- Look back over your response(s). How would you characterize your own beliefs and expectations about coaching a colleague?

Small-group discussion (10–15 minutes)

Ask participants to form groups of three to four people to share their written responses. They might exchange their writing or summarize their comments on the first three questions. Then, groups should discuss their own beliefs and expectations about coaching a colleague. By the conclusion of this discussion, participants should be prepared to share their ideas with the larger group.

The small- and large-group discussions of Maureen focus on the role of administrators in supporting and participating in coaching relationships. If you are facilitating a case experience with several administrators, you may want to expand this set of activities by adapting questions from earlier discussions. For example, how would Maureen explain her coaching role with Gina to another administrator? What seems to be most challenging for Maureen about this coaching role? What are Maureen's concerns about the coaching relationship between Pat and Gina?

Large-group discussion (25–35 minutes)

In the larger group, ask one person from each small group to report their responses. On newsprint, create a table of the types of coaching participants describe and a brief list of their features. Concentrate on identifying different approaches to coaching. Ask the small groups to briefly discuss with each other the strengths and weaknesses of the different approaches and then ask for volunteers to share their responses. If, by this point in the discussion, participants haven't shared their own expectations about coaching a colleague, ask them to do so.

Communicating Feedback

The central dilemma in the case relates to Gina and Pat's communication—in particular, whether and how Gina chooses to communicate feedback to Pat. Gina's decisions about what she communicates to Pat and how she communicates with Pat are tied to questions of expertise: What, as a coach, do I know and try to communicate to a colleague? What, as a coach, do I try to help a colleague learn for her- or himself? This set of activities focuses explicitly on the communication between Gina and Pat in the final scene. The first two activities offer a small-group analysis of the communication in the final scene and a large-group consideration of Gina's effectiveness in listening and in asserting her own perspective. This conversation should result in an understanding of what was effective overall and what could have been made more effective. The third activity offers an opportunity to analyze three possible responses Gina could have made to Pat's final question using the contents of the conversation about effectiveness as criteria for analyzing the responses. The last activity invites participants to respond to the question Pat poses at the end of the case.

Small-group discussion (20–30 minutes)

Ask participants to return to the case and reread the last scene. Then ask them, working in small groups of four (different from those in the previous activity), to consider the following questions:

■ What is Gina's approach in her conversation with Pat?
■ What are the strengths of the communication between Gina and Pat?
■ What are the weaknesses of their communication?
■ What suggestions would you make to Gina about changing her approach? Continuing with her approach?

Suggest that in each small group, one person take responsibility for noting the group's thinking about one question and then sharing the group's response in the following large-group discussion. In this way, each group member will have note-taking responsibility for one question.

The "Communicating Feedback" segment of the discussion is intended to raise issues around coaching as a leadership role. We believe that it complements professional development experiences related to developing peer-coaching skills, although it is not intended to represent the body of knowledge about peer coaching. As a result of this discussion, participants may identify the need for access to formal peer coaching training or resources. (See Robbins 1991, CEDR 1989, Garmston and Costa 1994, and Joyce and Showers 1988.)

The small-group analysis of the interchange between Gina and Pat will raise a number of issues. Some participants may claim that the primary reason for the communications problem is the absence of ground rules in Gina and Pat's work together. You may find the set of activities that follow "Considering Ground Rules" useful at this point in the case discussion. However, we see the issue as more than a lack of ground rules and suggest that you take some time with the "Communicating Feedback" activities. Even if a strong set of ground rules is established at the outset of a coaching relationship, specific communication skills are necessary to ensure a successful coaching experience.

Large-group discussion (15–20 minutes)

Ask participants to share their small-group discussions with the larger group by having one group member identify Gina's approach, a second identify a strength they have seen in Gina's and Pat's communication, a third identify a weakness in their communication, and a fourth offer a suggestion for Gina. Encourage participants to prepare a variety of responses to avoid duplication of ideas in the larger group.

Gina's role in the final scene includes both communicating her ideas to Pat and listening to Pat's experience and concerns. Ask participants to assess Gina's effectiveness first, as a listener in the conversation:

■ How effective is Gina as a listener in the conversation?
■ What evidence demonstrates Gina's effectiveness as a listener?

then in communicating feedback to Pat:

■ How effective is Gina in communicating her feedback to Pat?
■ What evidence in the case demonstrates her effectiveness?

Large-group discussion (20–30 minutes)

Direct participants' attention to Gina's dilemma at the end of the case. Pat asks, "What are you trying to say, Gina? I don't get where you're coming from. On the one hand, you say I'm doing fine, but on the other, it sounds as if you don't think it's going so well. What do you really think about how the unit is working?"

Gina could make several possible responses to Pat. Share the following possibilities with the large group, one at a time, on overhead transparencies.

"Truthfully, Pat, I don't think it's going very well. You're not really doing inquiry-based science."

"Pat, I think you're doing a terrific job, especially given that this is the first kit that you've taught. There's always room for improvement—I know there is in my science classes—but you are on the right track."

"I am concerned about the worksheet you used today. My concern is that it provided too much structure for the students. The terrarium activity was hands-on, but it didn't require the kids to do enough thinking about what ought to be in the terrarium and why. I don't think they learned very much about habitats from the activity."

Have participants consider each response, asking the following questions:

■ What are the strengths of this response?
■ What are the weaknesses of this response?
■ How would you expect Pat to respond next?

This combination of small-group discussion and reporting to the large group will prepare participants for the next set of questions, which look at specific examples of Gina's communication with Pat. In assessing Gina's effectiveness, insist that participants cite evidence from the case to back their claims. Using evidence offers other group members the chance to concur or to suggest alternative interpretations, contributing to a more productive discussion.

In preparing for this discussion, it will be useful to give some thought to the strengths and weaknesses of these three responses. The communication model offered below from McGonagill and Associates and Education Development Center, Inc. is intended to inform your thinking and facilitation, rather than for sharing with participants.

According to this model, feedback that fully expresses concerns while minimizing defensiveness should contain the following elements:

• *Concrete data: grounds the communication in observable data*

• *Impact: makes clear why you think this is important or what the consequences might be*

• *Tone of inquiry: communicates openness to hearing other people's point of view*

• *Feelings: conveys your own reaction or response*

Following we analyze the three responses, paying particular attention to these elements.

1. "Truthfully, Pat, . . ."

This response tells Pat Gina's true assessment of her teaching but does not help Pat learn anything. It communicates Gina's judgment, but not the reasoning behind that judgment. Analyzed according to the feedback model, this statement contains no concrete details and conveys no sense of why Gina is critical. In other words, it doesn't give Pat access to Gina's thought process, nor does it provide any indication of Gina's feelings.

2. "Pat, I think you're doing a terrific job, . . ."

This response provides Pat with some indication of Gina's feelings but does not tell her about Gina's concerns. Gina gives Pat no useful direction on how to improve what she is doing in the classroom. Pat might feel better temporarily—or she might not. This response might also backfire if Pat suspects that Gina is simply trying to make her feel better. In an effort to protect Pat's feelings, Gina is also "protecting" Pat from learning and undermining her own potential effectiveness as a coach.

3. "I am concerned . . ."

This response gives Pat concrete data about Gina's concern and her view of the impact of Pat's worksheet on students' learning. It allows Gina to share her feelings without making judgments. On the other hand, it does not offer Pat any information on how Gina feels she is doing overall. Some additional information that would frame the concern or put it in context might improve it ("Pat, I want to reassure you that things are going very well overall. I do have some concerns I would like to share with you . . .").

Remind participants of the earlier discussion in which they made recommendations to Gina about how to communicate more effectively. Those recommendations can serve as criteria for evaluating these responses.

Pair discussion (10–15 minutes)

Ask participants to work in pairs to compose their own responses to Pat's question. Suggest that they "test" their responses by having one person read the question and the other give his or her version of Gina's response. Have several participants copy their responses onto overhead transparencies for consideration by the rest of the group. As the pairs work, review the responses they have recorded.

Large-group discussion (15–25 minutes)

Ask the participants who have recorded a response on a transparency to lead the group in analyzing it using the previous questions about the strengths and weaknesses of each of Gina's proposed comments and Pat's expected response.

Considering Ground Rules

As relationships change, what constitutes appropriate interaction can become unclear. In these situations, taking the time to articulate rules for interacting can help relationships evolve more smoothly. The following set of activities addresses an aspect of Gina's coaching dilemma that is linked to her new relationship as a coach: unclear expectations held by Pat and Gina about what kinds of feedback will be offered, when it will be offered, and whether it will be considered and applied. Participants are asked to consider what procedures Gina and Pat should have established before they began their collaborative work together.

Large-group discussion (10–15 minutes)

The idea of establishing ground rules is likely to have come up in discussion, even in the less formal "maybe they should have figured out how to do this before they got to this point" kind of comment. This activity is intended to address that issue specifically. If it has already come up, you might say, "I'd like us to return to the issue of what Pat and Gina could have done ahead of time to prevent this situation and spend some time discussing that in detail."

Ask participants to consider this question:

■ What could Pat and Gina have done before Pat started teaching the unit to prepare to give and receive feedback?

Have participants generate some general ideas together as a whole group and record these ideas on an overhead transparency or newsprint for further exploration in the role play that follows.

Role play (30–40 minutes)

In this activity, participants role play a conversation between Pat and Gina as they set feedback ground rules. Participants work in groups of four divided into two pairs. In each pair, one person takes the role of Gina and the other person plays Pat. Participants are to role play a conversation between Pat and Gina before they begin co-teaching the science units, in which they talk about how the coaching relationship will proceed.

Remind participants of their earlier discussion of Pat's and Gina's concerns. Have each participant reflect silently on and then write about this question:

■ What do you think are your character's (Pat's or Gina's) three most important concerns about the coaching relationship?

Before starting the role play, ask the two "Pats" in the foursome to share their thoughts and then the two "Ginas." These reflections should form the basis for their role play.

In each pair, Gina will initiate the conversation with Pat, and they will work together to come up with "ground rules" for the coaching relationship. These procedures should describe when feedback will be given and in what form. Each "Pat and Gina" pair should record the ground rules they agree upon for observing and providing feedback. As the facilitator, you should circulate around the room and identify several different procedures. Have these pairs record their ground rules on overhead transparencies or on newsprint, or collect the ground rules and prepare a single transparency representing the group's work.

Large-group discussion (15–20 minutes)

In reporting to the larger group, have each pair (or selected pairs) present their ground rules and how they arrived at them. Ask the group to discuss their advantages and disadvantages:

■ How will they support Gina in giving feedback?
■ How will they support Pat in receiving and learning from feedback?
■ What are the risks in this strategy for Gina? for Pat?

Wrapping Up

This closing activity is designed to help participants arrive at some closure to their work with the case. Adapt the activity to fit the case experience you have constructed with participants. How you wrap up the case discussion and what you emphasize will depend on the purpose you have identified for this case experience.

Individual reflective writing (5–10 minutes)

Ask participants to review the various parts of the case experience by referring to their notes, worksheets, and any other artifacts from the discussion and to record their reflections on the following question: What insights into coaching colleagues have you gained as a result of this discussion?

Large-group discussion (10–15 minutes)

Ask participants to share their reflections on the insights they have gained into coaching colleagues. Point out ideas that speak to the two themes of this case: negotiating new relationships and developing expertise.

CHAPTER 2

Reaching Out

Case

Shirley Larson, Principal, Lincoln Elementary School
Roxanne Chantel, Fifth-grade teacher
Joyce Snow, Fifth-grade teacher
Roger Harris, Fourth-grade teacher
Pete Wagner, Fifth-grade teacher
Gwen Barry, Third-grade teacher
Leslie Haber, Second-grade teacher

Shirley Larson, the principal of Lincoln Elementary School, walked into the front office and went behind the counter to talk to the secretary, Carolyn Murphy. "Carolyn," she asked, pointing to an announcement, "does this say what I think it says?"

Carolyn took the sheet of paper and looked it over. "Roxanne wants to have an all-day science workshop for teachers."

"*Ten* of the teachers!" Shirley exclaimed incredulously. "That's half the staff. Roxanne and I discussed this briefly, but I had no idea she was talking about this many people. I can't believe she'd think this could work. Can we even cover them with subs?"

"I can dig around and find out," Carolyn replied.

"Well, see if it's possible. And let me know, will you?" Shirley walked back toward her office. "And I want to see Roxanne when she's free."

"Will do," replied Carolyn.

Roxanne Chantel, a fifth-grade teacher, had been teaching at Lincoln for nine years. Roxanne had been interested in science education since her college days, when she had taken several science education courses, and was enthusiastic about making improvements in the science program at Lincoln. Two years earlier, she and the two fourth-grade teachers, Joyce Snow and Roger Harris, had applied to be part of a new inquiry-based science program—and they had been accepted.

As part of the program, Roxanne, Joyce, and Roger attended a professional development program during the school year and summer, and they introduced the new inquiry-based approach to science in their classrooms. They were also using new science curriculum units consisting of kits with hands-on materials for students. Some units also required the use of technology, particularly computer graphing programs, so Roxanne, Joyce, and Roger had a few computers in their classrooms.

Shirley knew that Roxanne was eager to involve more teachers in using the kits and even more, in an inquiry-based approach to teaching. The all-day workshop was her way of getting more teachers involved. Roxanne was on a roll lately—getting Joyce and Roger involved, writing their successful application to the science program—and Shirley didn't want to dampen her enthusiasm. They certainly needed all the enthusiastic teachers at Lincoln they could get. But it wasn't just that, thought Shirley. She really agreed with the changes Roxanne was advocating. The science program at Lincoln, for the most part, didn't engage students in really *doing* science. Occasionally one of the teachers would try a more investigations-based unit on butterflies or animals, but the science in those units was not, Shirley suspected, very rigorous or thoughtful.

But this science workshop idea of Roxanne's would be an administrative nightmare. Having half the staff out of the building, even if they could get substitutes, meant that very few students would learn anything useful that day. The building would be in a state of chaos. It was hard enough when Roxanne, Joyce, and Roger were out of the building for a workshop. She would have to work out something else with Roxanne.

■ ■ ■

After school, Roxanne sat down with Joyce and Roger in her classroom. "Well, I talked with Shirley today about our request. It's not good news."

"She doesn't want us to do the workshop," Joyce stated flatly.

"Not exactly. She was real careful not to say that, and I believe her. Her concern was more the logistical issue of taking that many teachers out of the classroom on one day. So I suggested we do it on a

Saturday and pay people stipends. She wasn't sure she could afford that. She suggested that we start off slower and do something at the next faculty meeting. I managed to talk her into giving us a whole faculty meeting, so we would have an hour and a half after school next Tuesday afternoon."

"Well, that's better than nothing," remarked Joyce. "But that's not very much time. Especially if we want to get people involved actually doing the science themselves."

"And we'll have everyone there," added Roger, "rather than a small group. You know there are some people who aren't interested in trying a new approach to teaching science."

"Here's what I was thinking," Roxanne said. "I'm the one who is always preaching about science at faculty meetings. So I was thinking—what if you two presented this workshop instead of me, so that everyone will see that we're all interested in this? You could share an investigation from the electricity unit you're teaching, and they'd see how exciting and interesting the units are."

"Whoa!" said Roger. "I'm not sure I've got this inquiry approach down pat enough to model it for the whole staff! I'd want you to be up there with us."

"I'm saying I'd be there, but not as one of the presenters. You two have more credibility. People are tired of hearing from me—they think, 'Oh, that's just Roxanne going off about science again,' when I get up to talk about it!" Roxanne laughed.

Joyce shifted uneasily in her chair. "Roxanne, I just don't think Roger and I—no offense, Roger, maybe I should just speak for myself—I don't know the science as well as you do."

"Even if you don't," Roxanne declared, "and, by the way, I think that's debatable, but even if you don't, I think that sends a good message to everyone: you don't have to be trained in science to try these new units. Now let's figure out what we're going to do in that hour and a half."

■ ■ ■

Shirley Larson finished her announcements at the Tuesday faculty meeting in the library. "Now it's on with the agenda of the day. This afternoon's meeting is focused on science, and Joyce and Roger will lead a science activity and discussion of inquiry-based science. Joyce, Roger, and Roxanne have been working very hard on a special project on changing the way they teach science, and I'm really grateful that they've taken the time to prepare this for us today. So I'm going to turn the floor over to Joyce and Roger."

Roger began, "As you may know, Roxanne organized today's meeting to talk about new approaches to teaching science. We thought that to do that, we'd share with you what we've been doing with inquiry-based science in our classrooms. By doing an activity with you that we're using with our students, we thought you'd be able to get a better picture of what we mean by inquiry-based science."

Joyce continued. "We'd like to jump right in and get you actively involved in doing a science investigation. You'll be working at your tables, in groups of four, on an investigation called 'The Mystery Box,' from a unit on electricity that Roger and I are teaching to our fourth-graders right now. Each Mystery Box has several points labeled on it, marked by nails that are connected to whatever is in the box. We would like you to use the materials on the table at the back of the room—wires and bulbs—to construct circuits that will allow you to determine what's inside your box between each pair of points. In your small group, I'd like you to read through the investigation, and then try it yourselves. Roger is passing out a sheet that has the investigation written out, and another sheet for recording your results."

The teachers at each of the library tables began to collect their materials: a "Mystery Box," some wires, and a lightbulb. Joyce noticed that several of the teachers, including Pete Wagner, the other fifth-grade teacher, had not started on the task and seemed to be just sitting and chatting. She checked in quickly with Roger, and they decided to individually encourage each table to get going. They walked around to each group, explaining the investigation. Pete's group didn't seem too excited about the investigation but dutifully sent Gwen Barry, a third-grade teacher, to collect their materials. Maybe once they get started, thought Joyce, they'll get more excited about the investigation.

Joyce and Roger circulated among the groups, observing their investigations and clarifying the directions. For the most part, the groups worked industriously on the task, collecting their data, recording them, and making hypotheses about what was going on inside the Mystery Box. Roger and Joyce conferred at the front of the room.

Roger commented, "Most of the groups are really getting into this. It's taking longer than I thought, but that's okay with me as long as they're getting something from it. We might have to cut out the group presentations, though. What's going on in Pete's group, in the corner there?"

"Well," replied Joyce, "I don't want to seem like I'm hanging over their shoulders, nagging them to move along, so I haven't been over there in a while. They're doing something, although they don't look all that excited about it."

Roger nodded. "Let's give the groups a few more minutes to finish up. I think they're going to need it. Maybe that group will get moving if they know they don't have much time left."

Roger announced that there were ten minutes left for the small-group work. Joyce made her way over to Pete's group and asked what hypothesis they had come up with. Gwen responded in an offhand fashion, but Joyce could tell that the group wasn't very engaged in the investigation.

Roger flicked the lights off and on to get everyone's attention. "Thanks to all of the groups for their hard work on the investigation," he began. "Normally, in the classroom, we would have each group present their solution. However, we're running out of time, so we're going to skip over that part today. What we'd like to do now is to step away from the science activity a little bit and talk about how this approach to science could be used in the classroom."

Roger presented an overhead transparency listing the activities in the electricity unit and briefly explained each activity to the group. He paused and then added, "Joyce and I are convinced there's value in this approach to teaching. We would like to have others join us in using the kits and, what is more important, in using an inquiry-based approach to teaching science. So we'd like to hear from you what your thoughts are about it and any questions that you might have. What do you think of this approach?"

The teachers were silent for a moment. "So, let me understand this," Pete Wagner began. "The units are all activities like this one?"

"Well, not exactly like this one," said Roger, "but they all have the same general approach: some initial exploration in a topic like electricity, an investigation like the one we just did, and some reflection activities."

"Is there any textbook or anything for them to read? To get the science content they need?" Pete asked.

"Well, the idea is that the information comes out of the investigations," replied Roger. "Children aren't told the science; they discover it."

"So there's no textbook?" Pete asked again.

"No, there's not a textbook per se," Roger said. "Although in my classroom we have lots of science reference books, including some old textbooks, that the students use to look up information when they discover something they need to know."

"Okay, so there's no textbook. So, then my question is," Pete continued, "if kids are just 'discovering' little things all the time, how do you know what they're really learning? Kids are having fun with the materials, the batteries and wires and lightbulbs, but how do you know that they're really learning the science they need to know? Maybe that's okay for the little ones, but in the later grades they've got to start learning the science."

"They *do* learn the science. That I'm sure of," replied Roger emphatically. "It happens differently than in traditional units, but there's no question in my mind that they're learning the science, and I think they're learning it better than before."

"Actually, that relates to my question," Gwen Barry jumped in. "How do you grade these investigations? I'm not sure I could put a score on this work. I could score them on whether they were engaged in the investigation, but I wouldn't be able to tell what specifically they had learned in terms of the content."

"That's a hard one," Joyce responded. "Both Roger and I have been trying to figure out what kind of assessment to use and then how to translate it into a grade," said Joyce. "We've been trying to use more than one kind of assessment to figure out the full extent of what students know."

"I'm not really sure *I* even know what the science is in this investigation," laughed Leslie Haber, a second-grade teacher, "never mind teaching it."

"Actually, Leslie," said Joyce, "I'm glad you said that. I know just how you feel. I'm definitely not a science expert, and I've been learning the science right along with the kids."

Joyce noticed that Pete had raised his hand again. She scanned the room to see if anyone else had a question, but she didn't see any other hands, so she glanced back at him and said, "Pete?"

"I just want to know," Pete started, in a tone that Joyce thought was a little challenging, "where's the support for doing this sort of thing? You and Roger have special materials, you're out of school for workshops during the year, and you have computers. Is everyone going to get that kind of support?"

Joyce glanced at the clock as Pete was talking and realized they were out of time. Roger's eyes followed her gaze, and he noticed the time as well. "Pete, I'm not really sure how to answer that question," Roger said apologetically. "We're also out of time today. Maybe Shirley will let us take some time at the next meeting to address that question and any others that have come up. In the meantime, Joyce and I both thank you for your time and patience this afternoon."

The teachers clapped politely, stood up, and quickly began gathering their bags and coats.

■ ■ ■

After the teachers had left, Roger, Joyce, and Roxanne began collecting the Mystery Boxes, reorganizing the materials, and putting the chairs on top of the library tables.

Roger paused, holding a chair in his hands. "So what just happened here?" he demanded.

"What do you mean?" Roxanne looked puzzled. "I thought that went pretty well."

"My heart is still racing," said Joyce, shaking her head in amazement. "I'm all worked up. That was nerve-wracking! I'll take a group of children any time."

"Take a deep breath, Joyce," smiled Roxanne. "You were fine. What did you mean, Roger, when you asked 'What just happened'?"

"Well, Pete and Gwen were asking all those questions—I wasn't really sure what to say to them. My answers certainly didn't convince them that inquiry-based science is the way to go."

"Some people are just afraid of change," Roxanne explained. "Pete Wagner will always resist anything new. He always has, and that's not your fault. I should know—I've been talking with him about changing the way he does things until I'm blue in the face. There's nothing you can do to convince him."

Joyce looked troubled. "Pete's group really didn't try the activity. He didn't give the investigation a chance. Maybe if he had actually explored the science himself, he would have seen what we were talking about. I bet he was probably thinking, 'Who are they to come in here and tell me I have to do this activity?' And it's not as if I'm going to force him to do it."

Facilitator's Guide

Summary of the Case

The case opens as Shirley Larson, principal of Lincoln Elementary School, is considering a proposal for the faculty to participate in an all-day science workshop facilitated by three of Lincoln teachers: Roxanne Chantel, a fifth-grade teacher with a long-term interest in improving the science program at Lincoln, and Joyce Snow and Roger Harris, two fourth-grade teachers who have been involved in a professional-development science program with Roxanne. Shirley suggests a workshop for the other teachers at the next faculty meeting as an alternative to the full-day workshop. Roxanne agrees to the idea and meets with Joyce and Roger to propose that the two of them facilitate the inquiry-based science investigation they are currently working on in their fourth-grade classrooms. Joyce and Roger express concern about their relative lack of experience with the inquiry-based science approach, but they agree to facilitate the workshop anyway.

At the faculty meeting, Joyce and Roger involve teachers in the "Mystery Box" investigation from a science module focusing on electricity. While many of the teachers actively engage in the investigation, one group does not; this concerns Joyce and Roger, but they are not sure how to address it. In the whole-group discussion following the investigation, Pete Wagner and Gwen Barry (from the unengaged group) are persistent in their questions about how kids will learn the science content and how to assess and grade student work.

In the final scene, Joyce, Roger, and Roxanne share their impressions of the workshop. Roger is concerned that he was unable to answer the teachers' questions in a satisfactory fashion. Roxanne is convinced that Pete Wagner is simply resistant to all new ideas and not worth worrying about. Joyce is concerned that some teachers, including Pete, never really engaged with the science lesson. As the case ends, they are discussing their varied interpretations.

Leadership Themes

As teacher leaders take up the responsibility of teaching their colleagues through professional development, they encounter questions about their own expertise and about working with others who may be resistant to the message they carry or the role they play. This case portrays a group of teacher leaders taking on the role of instructors to help their colleagues develop a deeper understanding of science content and inquiry-based pedagogy. This group of teacher leaders grapples with issues about their leadership role both in the workshop they facilitate for their colleagues and in the preparation and debriefing work they do together.

In particular, the case offers the opportunity to explore questions about

- *Developing expertise:* What kind of content expertise do teacher leaders need to be effective? What kind of design, facilitation, and communication expertise do teacher leaders need to work with teachers as adult learners?
- *Dealing with resistant colleagues:* What does it mean when a teacher "resists" a new idea or innovation? How can a teacher leader respond?

Summary of Activities

This guide offers six sets of suggested activities designed to support discussion of the case. You should feel free to add or delete activities, adapt them to suit your purposes, or reorder the activities to fit the needs of participants. As presented here, the sets of activities are structured to focus first on the content of the case itself and then to consider larger issues beyond the immediate case scenario related to the leadership themes. Estimates of the total amount of time needed, if one were to do all the activities in a set, are given in parentheses below. Time estimates for individual activities are given in the descriptions that follow.

The six sets of activities are as follows:

- *Getting Started:* An individual activity along with pair and large-group discussions of the range and variety of the issues contained in the case (25–35 minutes)
- *Understanding Perspectives:* Small- and large-group discussions to consider the perspectives held by different characters supported by evidence (30–40 minutes)
- *Considering Expertise:* Large-group and triad discussions investigating the kinds of expertise teacher leaders need as instructors of their colleagues (50–65 minutes)
- *Exploring Resistance:* Small- and large-group discussions, role play, and individual reflections asking participants to consider the "resistance" experienced by the characters in the case, its origin, and possible facilitative responses (85–115 minutes)
- *Developing Expertise in Workshop Design:* A small-group activity followed by a large-group discussion offering an opportunity to step away from the case to design a workshop session (45–75 minutes)
- *Wrapping Up:* An individual written reflection followed by a large-group discussion about the kind of expertise teacher leaders need to instruct colleagues (15–25 minutes)

Getting Started

This initial discussion activity is intended to support participants in developing a common understanding of the range and variety of issues in the case. Discussion in this section encourages participants to reflect on their ideas about instructing colleagues and to articulate problems and issues in the case.

Individual reflection (5 minutes)

Before beginning, ask participants to write down their current ideas about the following question. Ask them to set this piece of writing aside until the end of the case experience, when they will have a chance to revisit and revise their ideas (see p. 52).

■ What kind of expertise do teacher leaders need in order to act as instructors of their colleagues?

Pair/square discussion (10–15 minutes)

Divide the group into pairs. Ask each participant, individually, to briefly summarize what happened in the case and then share that description with his or her partner. After both partners have had an opportunity to share, the pair then turns to another pair sitting close by and shares their descriptions with them. The "square" (four participants or two pairs) discusses the ways in which their descriptions are similar and different. You might use the following questions:

■ What are the key points in this story?
■ In what way is your description similar to mine? Different from mine?
■ Are the differences in our summaries critical? Do they get at different issues?

Large-group discussion (10–15 minutes)

Ask the "squares" to share their descriptions with others in the larger group. Begin by getting a full description from one square, and then ask subsequent squares to add their own ideas (if different from those already reported). Also, ask participants to note new ideas (things they hadn't thought of themselves but with which they readily agree), questions sparked by other participants' descriptions, and examples of how others' ideas have caused them to rethink and modify their own descriptions. Record these ideas on a sheet of newsprint divided into thirds. Label one section with a lightbulb to represent the "bright ideas" generated by the discussion; a second section with a series of question marks to note the questions participants want to track through the discussion; and a third section with a large triangle or delta to record changes or shifts in perspective on the case in this opening discussion.

Use the following questions to help participants share their descriptions in the larger group:

By posing the question about expertise, you are asking participants for their first thoughts about a major theme in the case. Use this written reflection as a way to get people thinking but don't begin the discussion here. Instead, explain that recording their ideas now will give them something to return to at the end of the discussion, to judge whether and how their thinking might have changed or been enlarged by the case experience. After participants finish writing, move directly into the next activity.

The list of bright ideas, questions, and changes in thinking is useful for focusing attention during the large-group discussion. The facilitator can ask participants to identify which type of comment is being made. After the large group has finished discussing the three sections, the pairs can meet again to discuss the kinds of issues recorded. If needed, there may be another round of large-group discussion to record additional bright ideas, burning questions, or shifts in thinking.

A natural pitfall for participants at this early point in the discussion is to want to offer solutions to the compelling dilemma at the end of the case. The challenge for the facilitator is to keep participants on track in describing the case and in identifying the issues they see in the case, rather than offering their ideas about how to address these issues. The focus is on defining problems rather than on problem solving.

The small-group discussion question is phrased in the first person to invite the groups to speak as the character they are focusing on as they consider what the character's intentions are for the workshop session. This device can help participants to keep the focus on the character's goals rather than on their own goals.

This set of questions also invites inquiry into the issue of evidence. Different characters will have varied interpretations of the success of the workshop, since they speak from their own impressions and limited observational data. Identifying the evidence each character draws on to determine if the purpose of the workshop has been met provides a springboard to a discussion of the need to collect specific data to help evaluate the success of professional development sessions.

- Do you have anything else to add to the description the first "square" offered?
- Does anyone want to comment on any of the new bright ideas they're hearing for the first time? What strikes you as interesting or important about these ideas?
- Are there any questions these descriptions are raising for you? What further discussion would you like to have before you return to these questions?
- Have any of you heard anything that is causing you to rethink your original description? What did you hear? What are you now thinking?

Understanding Perspectives

This activity combines small- and large-group discussion to explore the perspectives of the main characters in the case: Roxanne, Roger, Joyce, and Shirley. In particular, the discussion questions emphasize the different understanding each character has about the purpose of the workshop session at the faculty meeting and about the role and expertise of teacher leaders who act as instructors with colleagues.

Small-group discussion (15–20 minutes)

Working in groups of three or four, have participants reread the case, looking for evidence of how each of the four main characters (Roxanne, Roger, Joyce, and Shirley) would describe the purpose of the session held at the faculty meeting. There should be at least four small groups. Have each group choose one character to discuss or randomly assign a character to each group, making sure that the four main characters are covered. If there are more than four small groups, have more than one group consider Joyce and Roger, since they are the main characters in the case and the text contains more evidence of their perspectives. From the point of view of a single character, members of each small group should finish this statement:

- When teachers leave this session at the end of the faculty meeting, I really want them to know or be able to . . .

    Groups should also address the following questions:

- What evidence is there in the case of that intended purpose?
- How is that purpose reflected in the design and implementation of the session at the faculty meeting?
- What evidence is there that the purpose was met?

By focusing on the intended purpose of the workshop, participants have the opportunity to think about a critical issue for teacher leaders as instructors of their colleagues. In this role, teacher leaders often face the challenge of customizing workshop content and delivery to meet the needs of a particular group while remaining true to the purpose of the workshop.

Large-group discussion (15–20 minutes)

Have small groups present their answers to the above questions to the rest of the group. Ask the whole group to consider the following:

■ Do the characters agree on a common purpose? What are the similarities? What are the differences?

■ How does their agreement or disagreement affect the design and implementation of their session?

Considering Expertise

Roxanne, Joyce, and Roger could each be seen as taking on a leadership role as an instructor to their colleagues: that is, they intentionally act to support their colleagues' learning. The case offers evidence of each of their perspectives on what it means to be an instructor for their adult colleagues, and in particular offers evidence of their beliefs about the level of expertise needed by an instructor. For Roxanne, Joyce, Roger, and other teacher leaders, acting as an instructor means sorting through ideas and assumptions about their own capacity to take on that role. Sometimes this is framed as a ontent issues. Do I know enough about the content in this lesson/workshop/discussion to be able to help my colleagues learn? Sometimes this is framed as a process or teaching issue. Do I understand enough about how to help my colleagues, as adult learners, learn something from this lesson/workshop/discussion?

Large-group discussion (30–40 minutes)

In a large-group setting, ask participants to consider these questions:

■ How would Roxanne, Roger, and Joyce each characterize their roles as instructors? What would they describe as their responsibilities?

■ Do they believe they need to have a certain kind of expertise to carry out this role successfully?

■ If so, what expertise do they believe they need to have?

Moving away from the case, ask participants to consider the issue of expertise from their own perspective. Pose these two questions:

■ How is being an instructor with colleagues like being an instructor with children?

■ How is being an instructor with colleagues different from being an instructor with children?

The purpose of this activity is for participants to recognize that the instructional skills they have developed in teaching children transfer to teaching adults. At the same time, however, teaching adults also calls for particular skills.

The purpose of sharing out in the larger group is to get new views on the table. Each small group may come to consensus within the group, but hearing the perspective of another character (or another interpretation of their character), is likely to raise issues the small group hadn't considered earlier.

Linda Lambert (1998), in calling for a rethinking of leadership, states that it is "about learning together, and constructing meaning and knowledge collectively and collaboratively. It involves opportunities to surface and mediate perceptions, values, beliefs, information, and assumptions through continuing conversations . . . and to create actions that grow out of these new understandings" (pp. 5–6). Introducing different definitions of leadership and prompting dialogue to clarify participants' conceptions of teacher leadership may be a useful strategy at this juncture. See also CSE/ESIE (1997) and Lord (1994).

Depending on your objectives for the session, this is an opportunity to introduce or emphasize related topics, such as equity issues, adult learning theory, or research on learning styles.

In comparing the skills needed to teach children and those needed to teach adults, consider that adult learning typically provides:

- *opportunities for learners to shape the content of the workshops, institute courses, or seminars*

- *time for reflection, prediction, and exploration*

- *multiple modes of presentation and information processing*

- *support and feedback from people with expertise*

- *connections between new concepts and information and current knowledge and experience*

- *a safe environment to try new ideas and approaches (Regional Educational Laboratories 1995)*

See also Loucks-Horsley et al. (1998) and Garmston (1993).

Michael Fullan (1993, 1999, and Fullan and Stiegelbauer 1991) explores approaches to change and resistance in many of his books. Have resources such as these on a table for participants to peruse before or after the case discussion or during breaks. Put compelling quotes on an overhead transparency to pique participants' interest in exploring or borrowing resources. For example, display the following quote: "Resistance is an essential ingredient of progress. . . . 'Respecting those you wish to silence' is a good rule of thumb. You often learn more from people who disagree with you than you do from people who agree, but you underlisten to the former and overlisten to the latter" (1999, pp. 22–23).

Triad discussion (20–25 minutes)

Divide the group into triads. Create a Venn diagram with two intersecting sets: "Instructing Children" and "Instructing Adults," as in Figure 2.1. The task for each triad is to come to consensus on what they think should be represented on the Venn diagram in the three categories. During this discussion, have each member of the triad take notes on one set (i.e., one person takes notes on "Instructing Children," one on "Instructing Adults," and the third on the intersection of these two sets). Post three large sketches of the Venn diagram around the room (simply for convenience so that more people can be entering data simultaneously) and ask the each participant to record responses in the appropriate place on the diagram. After responses are recorded, have participants walk to the individual sections to note common and unique responses.

Exploring Resistance

In the final scene of the case, Roger, Roxanne, and Joyce discuss their varied interpretations of the workshop. One concern is their interactions with fifth-grade teacher Pete Wagner. Roxanne expresses her conviction that "Pete Wagner will always resist anything new. He always has, and that's not your fault. . . . There's nothing you can do to convince him." In the following large-group discussion activity, participants explore the idea of resistance focusing on possible interpretations of Pete's perspective offered by the case. A final activity gives participants an opportunity to reflect on resistant colleagues at their own schools and to consider approaches for interacting with them.

Pair and small-group discussion (20–30 minutes)

Ask participants to form pairs for discussion. Direct participants' attention to the final scene of the case. Ask them to consider the statements of Roxanne, Joyce, and Roger as the characters reflect on the workshop.

- What explanations do Roger, Roxanne, and Joyce each offer for Pete's behavior and his questions during the workshop?

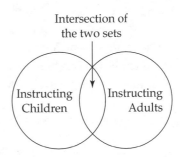

Figure 2.1: **Example of a Venn diagram**

After the pairs have had a chance to discuss their responses to this question, pose two additional questions:

- Do you agree with Roxanne that Pete "will always resist anything new. . . there's nothing you can do to convince him"? Why or why not?
- From your perspective, are Pete's concerns and questions legitimate? In what ways?

Ask participants to use a four-step interview process to help them address these questions in a thoughtful and considered way.

Step 1: One partner poses the questions to the other partner. The "interviewer" notes the partner's responses and asks clarifying questions as necessary.

Step 2: The other partner takes on the "interviewer" role, posing the questions, asking for clarification, and making notes on the other person's responses.

Step 3: The two partners join with another pair of participants, and each person shares her or his partner's views on the meaning of Pete's "resistance."

Step 4: The group of four summarizes their responses and appoints a spokesperson to communicate their thinking to the larger group.

Large-group discussion (15–20 minutes)

The spokesperson from each small group reports on the group's views on Pete's actions. If no one is willing to take Pete's point of view, the facilitator can make the request explicit: "Perhaps Pete has some legitimate concerns. Could someone articulate Pete's perspective?"

Role play (10–15 minutes)

To open up a discussion of Pete's perspective, you, the facilitator, could play Pete in a role-play situation and encourage participants to argue with "him." This gives you the chance to represent a possibly underrepresented or unconsidered perspective as legitimate, and to facilitate a discussion regarding its merits.

By taking on the role of Pete in this role play, you invite participants to take his point of view seriously and to hear and begin to speculate about the ideas that are important to him. It is easy to dismiss a colleague like Pete, and yet understanding what his resistance is about is key to trying to change his actions. This role play is a powerful strategy. Even if you tend to bypass such activities, we encourage you to consider what this role-play activity can contribute to the case experience.

As Pete, you might say something like this:

Hey, listen, I'm here, aren't I? What do you expect? That we're all going to follow you blindly and say, "Well, gee, since you're so

Groups may offer several interpretations of what "resistance" means. Here, we present several interpretations of Pete's resistance and their implications for Joyce and Roger. We offer this not for direct discussion but rather to help you, the facilitator, in your planning.

Roxanne suggests that Pete's resistance is a reaction to any change, and thus is unconnected to efforts Roger and Joyce may make to influence him. From her perspective, Pete's resistance is an aspect of his personality and not a reaction to the ideas offered. This approach discounts the possibility that Pete may have legitimate concerns from which something could be learned.

Another possible interpretation is that Pete needs to be convinced that inquiry-based science is the right way to go, and that Roger and Joyce have not yet made a convincing argument. This view implies that Roger and Joyce need to sharpen their argument so they can win Pete over. But this view also misses the opportunity to learn from Pete by listening to him.

A third interpretation could consider Pete's concerns legitimate from his vantage point, even though others may not share his point of view. This implies that Joyce and Roger need to listen carefully to Pete before they respond, perhaps even adapting future activities to accommodate Pete's needs. This approach might be less useful if Joyce and Roger spend too much time on Pete, to the detriment of other participants, or if he is unwilling to engage in discussion or reciprocate by listening to others.

gung ho, I guess I'll jump off the Brooklyn Bridge too!"? What have you shown me that proves this is the best approach for kids? So far, all I've seen is a neat activity that people get excited about because it's hands-on. What does that have to do with making sure kids are learning more? Don't treat me like I'm some sort of grumpy, stubborn old dog that you can dismiss just because I don't automatically agree with you.

You might continue the role play as Pete by responding to questions and comments from participants. This is an opportunity to demonstrate what can be learned in a dialogue with a colleague like Pete. It is also a chance to debrief the group about the conversation. As Pete, you can speak to some of the underlying concerns that might not have been articulated or taken seriously or to the proposed solutions that might not address central problems.

Ask other participants to take on the role of Pete and engage in the discussion. This helps to uncover issues and concerns that can explain Pete's resistance.

Large-group discussion (20–25 minutes)
Ask participants to turn their attention to the interactions among Roger, Joyce, Pete, and Gwen and give them time to reflect silently on this question:

- What is your assessment of how Joyce or Roger dealt with the lack of engagement shown by Pete and his group?

Direct participants' attention to the second half of the third scene in the case, where we see Roger interacting with Pete as Pete raises questions:

- How does Roger attempt to deal with Pete's questions?
- What else could Roger or Joyce have done?

Invite participants to share their thinking about Roger's interactions with Pete. Ask for specific evidence (What does Roger do?) as well as interpretation (What is your assessment of Roger's actions?). In addition, invite speculation (What else could Roger have done?). Explore with participants whether their views on Roger's actions are the same as their views on Joyce's actions.

If no one offers a critique of Roger's approach to Pete, you, as facilitator can question it directly: "I think you could make an argument that Roger contributes to Pete's frustration and confusion because, rather than listen to his concerns, he tries to answer them directly. Would anyone like to argue that point?"

Individual written reflection (10 minutes)

To extend the group's exploration of resistance and to support participants in transferring the ideas to their own school context, ask that they work silently and individually to address one or more of the following questions in writing:

- Is there someone you consider "resistant" to inquiry-based science on the faculty of your school?
- What do you believe are his or her concerns about teaching inquiry-based science?
- What evidence have you seen of those concerns?
- Have you made any attempts to influence him or her? If so, what was your approach? If not, why not?
- How would you approach this person in the future about inquiry-based science?

You might post these questions on newsprint or on an overhead transparency or print them on a worksheet to be distributed to participants.

Small-group discussion (10–15 minutes)

Once participants have reflected privately, group them according to the concerns they believe a "resistant" colleague might have. Ask them to talk, in round-robin style, about the approaches they have used thus far with such a colleague and if or how they might modify those approaches in light of the case discussion.

Developing Expertise in Workshop Design

As instructors of colleagues, most often in workshop settings, teacher leaders are called on to demonstrate their knowledge and skill in designing engaging and purposeful workshops. Some teacher leaders develop a particular kind of expertise through on-the-job experience, mentoring by accomplished teacher leaders, or skill building and other kinds of directed experience. In their own professional development designs teacher leaders usually adopt the same pedagogical approach they experienced in their own training, designing workshops that *tell* others, often in convincing and thoughtful ways, or workshops that *engage* others in a learning experience.

In this activity, participants step away from their direct interpretation of the case to address workshop design issues. Working in small groups, they design a workshop based on some of the information in the case. Their actions should be informed by earlier discussion of how the intended purpose of professional development influences the design of workshop sessions or other learning experiences for teachers.

For some people silent reflection is simply time to think. For others, it is time to write. For still others, the "silent" part of the reflection is challenging because they think best when they can talk through their ideas with others. Since there are few opportunities for silence in most discussion-based experiences, putting those who need to sort out their ideas by themselves at a disadvantage compared to those who think best in group situations, make an effort to enforce the silence. Assure those who would prefer to talk that there will be plenty of time to do just that afterward.

The facilitator should be alert to how participants are interpreting "expertise." Many will proceed to design a workshop in which they, as instructors, tell others what is worth knowing. This "telling" *mode may be appropriate for the intended purpose of their workshop, but this approach **may** be chosen because it feels safe. If I'm the expert, I should tell you what I know. Or, if I'm telling you what I know, I don't open the door to questions or issues about which I know very little or which make me feel uncomfortable. An alternative stance is to engage participants in exploring questions and issues, rather than to tell them what they should know. According to this approach, if I'm the expert, I should guide your inquiry so you can learn some things for yourself and pinpoint what else you want or need to learn. Again, this is a question of the intended purpose of the workshop. Take the opportunity to help participants see that they make choices in the design of professional development, including choosing what stance they take as an instructor, a stance that carries underlying assumptions about their own expertise.*

There is usually insufficient time for small groups to develop a full plan. Rather than plan the session minute by minute, encourage participants to outline it in a broad way or to indicate the kinds of activities that might take place. The small- and large-

Small-group discussion (30–45 minutes)

Participants will form small working groups by selecting one of the following three design challenges to address with two to three colleagues. Present and explain each challenge as needed, so that participants are clear about the design challenge they are selecting:

- Redesign challenge: Take on the task that Roxanne, Joyce, and Roger faced at the beginning of the case: designing an hour-and-a-half workshop session for the Lincoln Elementary School faculty. This challenge gives participants the opportunity to take what they've discussed and learned in the case discussion into account in designing an improved workshop from the outset.
- Next steps challenge: Take on the task of making the next steps, given the existing story line of the case. Imagine that Shirley offers Roxanne, Joyce, and Roger another hour and a half at a future faculty meeting. This challenge gives participants an opportunity to develop a design that follows up on the workshop portrayed in the case or addresses some of the problems raised by that workshop.
- Translation challenge: Take on the task of developing a workshop for faculty at your own school. This challenge gives participants the chance to design an hour-and-a-half workshop they might offer to the faculty at their school.

After reviewing the three challenges, participants select one and then form small working groups of two to three people. If necessary, more than one group can work on the same challenge. Try to mix groups so that participants experienced in designing and facilitating workshops are grouped with inexperienced participants.

For their chosen challenge, ask participants to consider the following:

- What is the purpose of the session? What are the goals of participants' learning?
- Who are the participants? What are their needs and interests? (For example, how many "Petes" will be in the group?)
- What expertise will you and your co-instructors be relying on this workshop?
- What plan can you draft to address the articulated purpose, given the intended participants and your expertise? What kind of activities might you design or use?

Ask the experienced participants to offer examples from their own workshop experience, particularly on the question of purpose, in order to help the small groups begin their work.

Large-group discussion (15–30 minutes)

Ask one or more groups to record their answers to these questions on newsprint and to give a two- or three-minute summary of their plans to the larger group. Ask both the presenters and the rest of the group to consider how well the design of the activities matches the described purpose.

Wrapping Up

This closing activity is designed to help participants arrive at some closure to their work with the case. Adapt the activity to fit the case experience you have constructed with participants. How you wrap up the case discussion and what you emphasize will depend on the purpose you have identified for this case experience.

Individual reflective writing (5–10 minutes)

Ask participants to write down their responses to this question:

- What kind of expertise do teacher leaders need in order to act as instructors of their colleagues?

After participants have had the chance to record their ideas, ask them to locate the paper on which they wrote their responses to the same question at the outset of the session (see p. 44) before any discussion of the case, and to compare their initial response to the one they have just written.

Large-group discussion (10–15 minutes)

Ask participants to share with the larger group whether their thinking has changed and to describe specifically what the changes are. You might use the following questions:

- What is different about the kind of expertise instructors need, in your initial response and in the one you have just written?
- Do you see this as an important difference?
- What aspect of the case discussion led to changes in your thinking?
- Do you, as a teacher leader, possess the kind of expertise you think is needed to act as an instructor of your colleagues? Can you get access to the experiences or resources you need to cultivate this expertise?

group discussions are more profitably spent reflecting on questions of purpose and expertise than on the particularities of a given design.

The large-group discussion activity can be modified in a number of ways. You could allocate additional time in small groups for more work on the workshop plan. You could also ask small groups who have taken on the same challenge to meet together to share their ideas, particularly on how they have articulated the purpose of their workshop. Reporting to the large group could then follow. In a somewhat more substantial variation, you could put participants into small groups only long enough for them to confirm their interpretation of their challenge, and then engage all the participants in some direct instruction about professional development design issues. For example, see Loucks-Horsley et al. (1998) or Joyce and Showers (1988). After a short period of discussion that focuses on purpose, or participants, or expertise, or some combination of issues, participants would then proceed to respond to the questions for their particular challenge and share their ideas with the large group, as described above.

CHAPTER 3

Making the Case

Case

Jack Dupree, Principal, Kennedy Elementary School
Angie Polcheck, First-grade teacher
Leo Wall, Fifth-grade teacher
Ron Winston, Parent
Marguerite Capuzzo, Third-grade teacher
Catherine Stempel, Second-grade teacher
Roberta Quindlen, Parent

"Thanks for joining us today," Jack Dupree said as he began the meeting. "As you know, I always appreciate your willingness to give up your time for meetings like these. The primary issue on our agenda today is the use of our professional time during this school year. We have set aside a half-day every month, when students are released early from school, for staff to work together. Last year, there were some concerns that we weren't spending this time well, that we were having sort of a hodgepodge of events—a workshop one month, then onto something else the next month. This group needs to set some priorities for what we do with that time together."

Jack had been the principal at Kennedy Elementary School for a year. The committee that had selected him for the position had been struck by his commitment to involving both teachers and parents in decisions made at the school. When the faculty had expressed concerns the previous year about the way professional time—the half-day per month—was being used, Jack had pulled together a volunteer group of teachers and two parent representatives to design a better plan for using this year's professional time. Gathered around a table in the library, in the late afternoon on this warm August day right before the start of school were teachers Angie Polcheck, Leo Wall, Marguerite Capuzzo, and Catherine Stempel, as well as Kennedy parents Ron Winston and Roberta Quindlen.

Angie Polcheck, a first-grade teacher, raised her hand "Excuse me, Jack. Could you review for us what some of our options are? I'm not sure what we could decide here today."

"Sure thing," replied Jack. "Basically, the way I see it, there are a lot of alternatives open to us. We could use the time to plan some changes we want to make at the school or to learn more about something new together. We could plan workshops where we bring in somebody from the outside, or we could work on something of our own here. There are some budget limitations, of course, if we are thinking of anything expensive." He smiled and looked around the table. "As you all know by now, I feel strongly that teachers and parents need to have input into these kinds of decisions, so I feel the decision is truly up to this group. My only strong preference is that the time not be spent as regular planning time, but that we use it to help us move on something that is a priority for us."

Leo Wall, a fifth-grade teacher, leaned toward the table. "Marguerite and I have some good ideas about expanding the inquiry-based science program we've been working on." He glanced over at Marguerite Capuzzo, and she nodded in agreement.

Ron Winston responded immediately, "My daughter Samantha was in Marguerite's third-grade class last year and got a lot out of that science program and the kits they were using. But I think, if we're going to keep the program going, then it's got to be in all the classrooms. What she learned last year in science is now going to waste in fourth grade, because it's all reading in the textbook. Maybe the kids are benefiting from that, too, but Samantha wasn't prepared for it, and she's not building on what she learned last year. Science meant one thing last year, and this year, it's something else."

"The fourth-grade classes are taking really different approaches," Leo agreed. "When last year's fourth-graders became my fifth-graders this year, some were already into hands-on work: asking questions, exploring, designing experiments. They were used to handling the science materials, working in groups, even organizing data. But for some of the kids, just working in long blocks of time on science was new. The first couple of months weren't so productive, because first I had to get everyone oriented to what we were doing."

"Okay, so it sounds like one proposal on the table is that we spend some time bringing this program up to full scale, doing some training with everyone, and working on implementing the science kits." Jack looked around the table for agreement.

Leo nodded. "That's what I'm suggesting."

"We were thinking," Marguerite added, "of having some workshop time early on in the year to learn about inquiry-based science teaching and the new science curriculum kits, and then asking everyone to try one kit in their classrooms. We would use the other days, later in the year, for grade-level partners to plan together and talk about how it's going."

"And use all the professional days on that? On the science kits?" asked Angie.

"Well, that's the idea we had," Marguerite replied, "to really focus the time on one thing that's worthwhile and important."

Catherine Stempel, a second-grade teacher, and Angie began speaking at once. They looked at each other, and Catherine gestured for Angie to go first. "Thanks," said Angie. "In my classroom, I'm really focused on getting students reading and writing and thinking about numbers and how they relate. We do some science, but it's not my number-one priority, and just because some people are involved in a special science project doesn't mean it's a priority for me."

"I understand your concern about reading and math," Leo started, "but, Marguerite, and Jeff O'Brien, and I have been working for years on this science stuff, and it's not some nice little project. It's meant to change the whole school eventually. Jack's been on board since he came last year, right, Jack?"

"You know I'm always supportive of teachers' efforts to improve their teaching and curriculum," replied Jack. "But this is a decision the whole group has to make."

"I agree with Angie," said Catherine. "You're talking about a huge commitment by all the teachers, and I really don't think that's the way I want us to spend all the professional time. I think we should put our money on our biggest priorities right now: reading and math. We've got to put first things first."

Leo leaned across the table toward the others. "All kids need to be literate in science, just as they do in reading and math. They are going to need to learn science to compete in the global marketplace, to eventually get jobs in science and technology. If we really want to be preparing kids for their futures, they have to be able to study science later on, and if they never have science now, they won't be able to do that."

There was a brief silence. Roberta Quindlen, another parent, responded slowly, "I'm thinking about what Catherine said. If kids can't read and write and do math, then I'm not sure they're going to be able to study the science later on anyway. Seems to me we should spend our money on the basics. I think if you were to ask other parents, they would say the same thing."

"Science *is* a basic," Leo replied excitedly. "I think it's really basic to any kid's success in the future. Look, the fact of the matter is that some of our kids get a good understanding of science, and some of them don't. It's an equity issue. Some of our kids only get a good science background because of what they do at home with their parents. We're not serving all kids well with our science curriculum the way it is."

Catherine frowned in frustration. "What I'm saying about reading and math makes it an equity issue, too, and I think it's a pretty important one. If kids can't master the basics, they won't be able to survive." She paused, looking directly at Leo. "Now Leo, I'm not saying we shouldn't teach science. I'm just saying we really need to look at our priorities."

"Science has *got* to be a priority!" Leo pounded his fist on the table. "When exactly is it going to be a priority? If we keep waiting until we're doing reading and math perfectly, we'll never get to science. In some classrooms at Kennedy, and you all know this, science isn't even taught at all."

There was an uncomfortable silence around the table after Leo's comments. Jack finally said, "Would anyone else like to comment or offer an opinion?"

"Marguerite, help me out here," Leo looked at her beseechingly.

Marguerite paused. "I guess I'm not sure what to say. I'm really happy with what kids in my class are learning, and I'd like to see more people using the kits and the inquiry-based approach. But obviously this group doesn't feel that's a priority right now, and I don't know that we can do anything about that. I guess we should hold off on expanding to the whole school until it's a priority for everyone."

Facilitator's Guide

Summary of the Case

Jack Dupree has been the principal at Kennedy Elementary School for one year and is known for his commitment to involving both teachers and students in decision making. Now it is August, and he has assembled a group of teachers and two parent representatives to discuss the use of "professional days," or student-free half days.

Leo Wall, a fifth-grade teacher and member of the committee, has been using a new inquiry-based science program in his classroom; he proposes using the professional days to advance the new science program. But several other committee members, who argue that mathematics and reading should be higher priorities, oppose his idea. Leo continues to make an impassioned case for the science program, offering arguments based on the need for science literacy, children's ability to take higher-level science courses and compete for jobs in the global marketplace, and equity in opportunities related to science.

He appeals to Marguerite Cappuzo, a fellow teacher also involved in the new science project, for support for his argument. Marguerite expresses her disappointment that the group doesn't see the science program as a priority, and suggests that they wait to expand the program until later.

Leadership Themes

This case focuses on issues of advocacy, conventionally defined as "arguing for and recommending a particular cause, proposal, or course of action." Teacher leaders are called upon or expected to act as advocates for reform efforts, often without an opportunity to reflect on what that role entails or to develop strategies that would help them be effective advocates. In this case, Leo provides an example of someone advocating for a particular point of view and, in fact, for a particular decision and set of actions by the group.

This case offers the opportunity for discussions around

- *Developing a critical mass for change:* What is meant by advocacy, as practiced by teacher leaders? How do we judge its effectiveness?
- *Building support among administrators:* What strategies might be used to build support among various individuals, including administrators? What are the intended outcomes of these efforts?

Summary of Activities

This guide offers six sets of suggested activities to support discussion of the case. You should feel free to add or delete activities, adapt them to suit your purposes, or resequence them to fit the needs of the group with which you will be working. As presented here, the sets of activities are structured to focus first on the content of the case itself and then to consider larger issues beyond the immediate case scenario related to the leadership themes. Estimates of the total amount of time needed, if one were to do all the activities in a set, are given in parentheses below. Time estimates for individual activities are given in the descriptions that follow.

The six sets of activities are as follows:

- *Getting Started:* Small- and large-group discussions of the range and variety of the issues contained in the case (20–30 minutes)
- *Understanding Perspectives:* Discussion in pairs, small groups, and large group supporting the exploration of the perspectives represented in the case, including use of professional days and characters' understanding of their roles (95–125 minutes)
- *Advocating for Change:* Large- and small-group discussions combined with reflection activities that ask participants to consider the advocacy role Leo takes on (80–105 minutes)
- *Building Support:* Small-group and individual reflection activities exploring how Leo might build support for his proposal and point of view, and encouraging participants to step away from the case using a similar series of questions to think about building support for their own work (55–90 minutes)
- *Focusing on the Principal's Role:* Pair and large-group discussions exploring the role of the principal as a facilitator and an advocate (25–35 minutes)
- *Wrapping Up:* Individual written reflection followed by pair and large-group discussions about features of effective advocacy and strategies for building support (25–40 minutes)

Getting Started

This initial discussion activity is intended to support participants in developing a common understanding of the range and variety of issues in the case. Discussion encourages participants to articulate problems and issues in the case.

Pair and small-group discussions (10–15 minutes)

Ask participants to pair up for a four-step interview.

Step 1: One partner asks the other to summarize the case and identify the key issues. The "interviewer" notes the partner's responses and asks clarifying questions as necessary.

Step 2: The other partner takes on the "interviewer" role, asking for a summary of the case and identification of key issues, seeking clarification, and making notes of the other person's responses.

Step 3: The two partners combine with another pair of participants and share their responses in round-robin style, each person sharing the summary and key issues of the case as stated by his or her partner.

Step 4: The group of four summarizes their responses and appoints a spokesperson to communicate their thinking to the larger group.

Large-group discussion (10–15 minutes)

Ask the spokesperson from each group of four to present their group's ideas to everyone. Encourage participants to note places where their summary or list of key issues is both similar to and different from others.

- What happened in the case?
- What are the key issues raised by the case?

Use the list of key issues raised by the case to frame the particular issues that you want participants to focus on in this case experience. This is also a good time to lay out the agenda for the entire case experience so that participants have a map of how the issues will be addressed.

Understanding Perspectives

This activity provides an opportunity for participants to become clear on the perspectives represented by the various characters in the case. The discussion questions below address two kinds of perspectives: perspectives related to the use of professional days which are made explicit in the case, and implicit perspectives of the characters about their roles in the group and in the conversation represented in the case.

There are too many characters in this case to do an exhaustive study of each one. We recommend that as the facilitator, you choose two to four characters to discuss. Leo, Marguerite, Jack, and Catherine are good choices for analysis because they offer a range of perspectives and because the case offers more evidence of their perspectives.

Small-group discussion (30–40 minutes)

Ask participants to form groups of four. These can be different from the ones they were in for the opening activity. Pose the following questions:

- How would each of these characters describe the problem in the case?
- What is the evidence in the case that supports your analysis?

Ask that each member of the foursome represent one character: Leo, Marguerite, Jack, or Catherine. Give participants time to consider the questions individually and ask them to take notes on their responses relative to their character.

Now reconfigure the groups so that all those representing Leo are together in a new group, all those representing Marguerite are together in another group, and so on. Do not form groups larger than four people. If necessary, create two or more Leo groups or two or more Marguerite groups to ensure that all participants have the chance to talk with others in their group. Participants have now formed "expert groups"—groups in which each member has had a chance to reflect on and discuss the same character. Ask participants in these expert groups to examine the evidence of the case and come up with a common interpretation of the problem from their character's (e.g., Leo's) point of view. In addition, participants should assess how the character feels about the problem. They should practice speaking in the first person, getting themselves in character for when they return to the original foursome to "become" that person. The same process (examining the evidence, creating a common interpretation, assessing the character's feelings, and getting into character) should be used by the Marguerite, Jack, and Catherine expert groups.

Participants return to their original foursome and each one speaks in the first person (as Leo or Marguerite, etc.) as he or she shares the description of the problem and the feelings connected to that problem. If challenged by others who disagree with the analysis of the character, the participant should refer to the evidence generated by the expert group.

Large-group discussion (30–40 minutes)

Begin the large-group discussion with Leo's perspective. The responses you get should now be those generated in the expert groups and refined in the original foursomes. Ask the question:

- What does Leo believe the problem is?

Record brief versions of the responses on the overhead or newsprint. Divide the paper or overhead in half lengthwise so that the problem description can appear on the left and the corresponding feelings (see next question) on the right. If disagreements or differences in interpretation arise, ask participants to note evidence from the case that supports the analysis.

Then, ask the group to consider the following question:

- How is Leo feeling? Why?

On the right side of the overhead or newsprint, add adjectives or phrases that describe Leo's feelings. Conversation about the character's feelings can provide additional insight into the character's perspective and can be a useful strategy for uncovering different interpretations of the same character.

When you have finished discussing Leo, look at the other characters in a similar manner. First discuss what the problem was from the character's perspective and then briefly discuss how the character was feeling. Continue to record responses on the overhead or newsprint.

One of the subtle ways that facilitation of this case can affect participants' perspective of advocacy is by creating an environment in which they can practice listening to, understanding, and validating different perspectives. This activity provides an extended opportunity to analyze the case from one character's perspective and then articulate that perspective so that others understand it, whether or not the participant agrees with that perspective.

Pair discussion (20–25 minutes)
This activity encourages participants to analyze the reasons—individual and collective—why members of a committee, a task force, or a working group are involved in that particular assembly. It also helps participants consider the impact group members expect to have on others. The purpose of this activity is to identify and discuss the underlying mindset or beliefs about working in groups. It gives participants an opportunity to think about how beliefs about roles in a group influence behavior in that group.

To begin, ask participants to reflect individually on a group they have been a part of—a school committee, a civic board, a church group, or some other assembly. Discuss with a partner the following questions:

■ What mindset or belief did you have about your role in the group?
■ Did this mindset affect your behavior in the group? In what ways?

You may need to offer a few additional questions to help the pairs start their discussion. For example:

■ Why were you a part of this group?
■ What did you expect to contribute? What did others expect you to contribute?
■ What did you do in this group?
■ Did your actions match your expectations?

Remind the pairs that they are trying to understand the relationship between perceived role and behavior in a group.

Then, ask participants to infer from the case which possible mindsets or beliefs Leo, Marguerite, Jack, and Catherine hold about their role in the committee discussion. These may be beliefs about who has authority in the group, what the role of conflict or disagreement is in the group, or whose views he or she is representing. The range of issues will vary. If there are particular issues that interest you, as facilitator, adapt the following prompts to address them:

■ Complete the following sentences for a given character:
  My role in the discussion is to . . .
  In this group, I am a person who . . .
■ How does that mindset influence the character's behavior in the case?
■ Does it limit the character?
■ Does it help or serve the character?

You might ask the pairs to respond to these questions for each of the four main characters. Or, you might ask participants to move back into their expert groups (for example, all the Leos together) to discuss the questions and then move into their foursomes (one Leo, one Marguerite, etc.) to share responses from the point of view of their character in preparation for reporting to the large group.

Large-group discussion (15–20 minutes)

This is another opportunity for participants to make clear the evidence they see in the case as well as to hear how others interpret the same information. Again, begin the sharing process by discussing Leo and then continue with the other characters. Ask participants for beliefs they inferred about Leo. If necessary, use responses to the sentence prompts (My role in the discussion is to . . . , In this group, I am a person who . . .) as a prelude for considering beliefs about roles within groups.

- How did the mindset influence Leo's behavior?
- How does the mindset limit and serve Leo?

It is likely that this discussion will raise issues related to the advocate role Leo plays in the case and may raise questions about the roles of other group members in relation to advocacy. In this way, the discussion will serve as a precursor to the following activity, which focuses on effective advocacy.

Advocating for Change

Teacher leaders are often called upon to be advocates for reform efforts. This advocacy can take the form of public spokesperson, informal supporter, or even strategic interventionist. The advocate role is important because through advocacy, a teacher leader can enlist others to join in or to promote a reform effort and, in this way, build the necessary critical mass to bring about change. This activity focuses on the role Leo plays as an advocate for inquiry-based science education and his effectiveness in that role. Leo's advocacy role is contrasted with that of Marguerite to help participants further explore what it means to advocate for change.

Large-group discussion (15–20 minutes)

Ask participants to think about what advocates do and mentally list verbs that describe the work of an advocate. In groups of four or five at a table or in a circle, ask one participant to begin by writing a verb from his or her mental list on a piece of paper and passing the paper to the person on their right. This is a silent activity. The paper travels around the group, each person adding a verb. After the paper has traveled around the group three or four times, call stop (a bit like the game of musical chairs). Ask the person holding the paper when you called stop in each group to stand up. Reading from his or her group's list, each standing person contributes one verb at a time, round-robin fashion, to a class list being written on newsprint, making sure not to repeat verbs. When the lists have been recorded completely, have the

You may need to prompt participants to focus on the actions of advocates. For example, you could ask them to brainstorm a few verbs that would follow the noun "advocates." Or, you could say, "We're filling in the blank here. Advocates [blank]. What verbs would you use to describe what advocates do?" If necessary, you can encourage participants by offering a dictionary definition of advocacy as speaking in favor of, arguing for a cause, or pleading in another's behalf. You can provide synonyms for advocate found in a thesaurus: support, promote, sponsor, or encourage. You can offer examples from real life by citing or asking for names of individuals who are advocates and then identifying verbs that typify their actions as advocates.

Usually, participants offer many verbs that frame advocacy as presentation or persuasion (e.g., convince, argue, tell). By contrast, few verbs on the list frame advocacy as listening to or understanding another's perspective (e.g., include, elicit, encourage). Pointing out different conceptions of advocacy (or introducing a few new verbs into the discussion) are ways in which the facilitator can help participants reflect on the meaning of advocacy.

Productive advocacy (Action Design Associates, 1996) means making your views known and building in others an understanding of those views in ways that maximize their potential influence and minimize defensiveness.

• **State your view.** *Leo does offer a viewpoint in the case and makes several attempts to make this view known.*

• **Provide the data upon which you base your view and make explicit how you get from these data to your conclusions.** *Although Leo is quite clear that he supports the expansion of the program and make claims about the effects of using the science curriculum, he does not share the thinking that leads him to believe in its effectiveness. In fact, he shares relatively little information about the program's approach, and does not communicate the connection he sees between the program and its potential impact. In the group discussion, Leo supports and defends his position, instead of helping others to understand the interests and experiences behind that position.*

• **Combine advocacy with inquiry.** *Leo is primarily concerned with being heard. He wants others to hear, understand, and agree with his position. He attempts to persuade them of the "rightness" of his position by repeatedly offering new arguments appealing to logic, emotion, and force to make his argument.*

larger group look for categories of verbs and discuss shared conceptions about advocacy.

Small-group discussion (15–20 minutes)

Each small group should identify Leo's approach to advocacy and analyze its advantages and disadvantages by addressing the following questions:

- Looking at the list of verbs created in the previous activity, which of them apply to Leo and his approach to advocacy?
- What is Leo advocating for in the case?
- How does he advocate for it? What is his strategy?
- What are the advantages of such a strategy?
- What are the disadvantages?

Large-group discussion (15–20 minutes)

Ask participants to report on their small-group discussions by offering their description of Leo's approach, and one advantage and one disadvantage they have identified. Keep a running list of the advantages and disadvantages of Leo's approach on two pieces of newsprint. If you have access to two newsprint easels, place them side by side and ask two participants to write down ideas as you facilitate the discussion.

Small-group discussion (15–20 minutes)

Ask participants to continue their small-group discussions and consider Marguerite as an advocate. Have them respond to the following questions:

- Is Marguerite an advocate for inquiry-based science? Why or why not?
- How does her approach in the committee discussion differ from Leo's?
- What are the advantages and disadvantages of Marguerite's approach?

In preparation for the large-group discussion, ask half of the small groups to argue that Marguerite is an advocate using evidence from the case. Assign the other half to argue the position that Marguerite is not an advocate, again using evidence from the case.

Large-group discussion (20–25 minutes)

Ask members of the small groups to report on their discussions to the larger group, alternating arguments for and against Marguerite as an advocate.

After considering both Leo and Marguerite as advocates, ask participants to reflect on the features of effective advocacy. Give participants two or three minutes, individually and silently, to write down several features of effective advocacy. Then, move to a large-group discussion of those features, asking participants for contributions and, on the overhead or on newsprint, forming a list of the features of effective advocacy.

Building Support

Teacher leaders build support for their work in a number of ways, most often by trying to persuade others of the logic or brilliance or moral certainty of one's position. Yet this stance is not as successful as we would like. More often than not, those we are trying to persuade are attempting to do the same: persuade *us* of the logic, brilliance, and moral certainty of *their* ideas. This can easily lead to a pattern of assertions and counterassertions that achieve little progress or understanding.

Building support can be achieved, however, by understanding the interests of others and using that understanding to find common ground. This means taking seriously the ideas others are advocating, working to figure out their underlying interests and assumptions, and actively exploring ways in which these ideas are or could be connected to one's own ideas. This is the work of finding common ground, a much more stable place on which to build support for ideas and actions than individual dominance.

There is no evidence in the case that Leo is attempting to understand the perspectives of other group members or working to find common ground among perspectives. Leo answers each concern raised by those on the committee who oppose his plan with a counterargument rather than with an inquiry-based response to elicit their thinking, a strategy that would help the group to build the mutual understanding that could move them forward.

This activity is an opportunity for participants to explore various ways in which Leo might be a more successful advocate. By trying to understand the interests of others and not simply saying essentially the same thing over and over, Leo can build support for issues that turn out to be important to him *and* to others.

This activity asks participants to step away from the data of the case and to consider how Leo could build support for his ideas and proposals among other committee members. Finding common ground is a useful strategy for building support and involves inquiring about and understanding the interests and concerns that others have. This knowledge is important in finding a space in which both parties' interests might be met. After considering ways in which Leo might build support among his colleagues, ask participants to consider their roles as advocates in their own school contexts using similar questions for analysis.

Small-group discussion (20–30 minutes)

Ask participants to form new small groups to consider the different strategies Leo may need to pursue to build support for his ideas with

The large-group discussion contrasting Leo and Marguerite is another opportunity to articulate a view of advocacy as more than "marketing" an idea. Phillip Schlechty (1991) underscores the need for leaders to be more than "old-style salesmen." What a colleague wants "is to be assured that he or she is an honored participant (rather than a pawn to be manipulated), a respected intellect deserving of support and, most of all, a valued colleague" (p. 95). Taking such an advocacy stance with valued colleagues means that one must take seriously their point of view and actively inquire into their thinking. Robert Garmston and Bruce Wellman (1998) note that "of all the norms, balancing advocacy and inquiry requires the most cognitive, emotional and moral sophistication and creates the most profound shifts in group thinking and relationships" (p. 33).

different individuals (Jack, Marguerite, and Ron might require different strategies than Catherine, Angie, and Roberta). You may want to include these questions on a printed reflection sheet for groups to work with:

- As an advocate, what is Leo's primary interest in this meeting?
- With which members of the committee does he need to build support for that interest? (Choose one or two characters on whom to focus.)
- What is that person's primary interest? How is it similar to and different from Leo's?
- What is the nature of Leo's relationship to that person?
- What strategies should Leo use to build support for his interests with that person?

Large-group discussion (20–40 minutes)

Identify the other character(s) that each small group discussed as individuals with whom Leo needs to build support. For example, if one or more groups discussed Catherine, begin the discussion by asking these groups to describe Leo's primary interest in this meeting. Then continue to discuss the other questions above, considering Catherine's interest, her relationship with Leo, and alternative strategies Leo could employ to gain her support. Continue in the same way, discussing other characters with whom Leo needs to build support. Begin again by asking about Leo's interests. It's likely that how a group identifies Leo's interests will shift somewhat in relationship to a particular character and his or her interests.

Consider asking participants to role play Leo in order to try out different strategies for building support. One person, acting as Leo, might interact with Catherine, for example, by asking her direct questions about her ideas or testing out his understanding of her concerns. Another "Leo" might interact with another "Catherine" by discussing how he is interpreting Catherine's comments and exploring the ways in which Catherine's concerns seem to be similar to his own. By witnessing a variety of role plays, participants can start to see how different strategies might be used to build support, which increases the likelihood that they might try one of them in the future.

Individual reflection (15–20 minutes)

Ask participants to imagine themselves as advocates for inquiry-based science and have them reflect on their own efforts to build support with colleagues, using the following questions (similar to those above):

- What are you primarily interested in advocating for?
- Who are the key stakeholders in that situation? Choose one or two and identify their primary interests. Who else is involved?

- What strategies might you adopt in building support for your interests among these stakeholders?

You may have participants pair up to discuss their reflections or ask that a few volunteers share their ideas in a large-group discussion.

Focusing on the Principal's Role

Principals can be the most important advocates for change within a school, because of the authority and power they wield in the building or even because they are members of teacher leader teams within a school. It is critical that teacher leaders seek their support for change efforts. Jack Dupree, the principal in the case, plays an almost silent role in the discussion. He offers some framing of the meeting up front and an explanation of the possibilities for group decision making. When Leo calls upon him to offer an opinion on expanding the science program, however, he demurs, saying instead: "You know I'm always supportive of teachers' efforts to improve their teaching and curriculum," replied Jack. "But this is a decision the whole group has to make."

In the case, we see evidence of Jack's involvement in the conversation at only two other points: when he summarizes Leo's proposal and, after Leo has spoken, when he asks whether anyone else would like to "comment or offer an opinion." One could argue that Jack is attempting to be a neutral facilitator of the group.

Pair discussion (10–15 minutes)

Ask participants to form pairs and consider Jack's role in the group by responding to the following questions:

- What is Jack's strategy in the meeting?
- What are the benefits and risks of such a strategy?
- Should Jack have made a different move at some point in the discussion? What, if anything, should he have done differently? Why?

Large-group discussion (15–20 minutes)

Bring the pairs together in the larger group to share their perceptions of Jack's role. Consider these questions:

- Was Jack effective? Why or why not?
- Was Jack an advocate? What data from the case support your response?
- Given your perspective on Jack as an advocate, what might Leo have done before the meeting to gain Jack's support? What might Leo have done during the meeting? After the meeting?

Wrapping Up

This closing activity is designed to help participants arrive at some closure to their work with the case. Adapt the activity to fit the case

This set of activities is particularly useful when principals are participants in a case experience or in situations where questions or concerns about the principal's role are raised. They highlight the role of the principal as an advocate and provide participants extended opportunities to consider principals' perspective and actions.

experience you have constructed with participants. How you wrap up the case discussion and what you emphasize will depend on the purpose you have identified for this case experience.

Individual written reflection (5–10 minutes)

Ask participants to reflect in writing on two topics:

1. Features of effective advocacy
2. Strategies for building support

Pair discussion (10–15 minutes)

Ask participants to select one of the two topics they have written about and be prepared to articulate their ideas on that topic to a partner. Have those who selected the first topic hold up one finger and those who selected the second topic hold up two fingers. Ask people who have selected the same topics to pair up, encouraging participants to partner with someone they do not know well or with whom they have not yet worked.

Ask one person in the pair to begin by expressing his or her ideas on the selected topic. The other person can assist by paraphrasing what he or she has heard and asking clarifying questions. Partners then switch roles.

Large-group discussion (10–15 minutes)

Draw the pairs back together into the larger group and ask each participant to contribute one idea he or she has learned from the partner about the selected topic. Participants might complete a statement such as "Susan helped me to understand . . ." Continue until each participant feels that an idea important to his or her own thinking has been articulated for the larger group.

CHAPTER 4

Specialist for All Seasons

Case

Anne Alexander, Mathematics specialist, Roosevelt Elementary School
Vivian Snyder, Principal
Claire Lindgren, Director of instruction, Northfield Public Schools

Late Monday Afternoon

Anne Alexander hooked the heavy door of Roosevelt Elementary
School with her thumb and finger and inched it open, her hands full
of bags of mathematics resource materials. She entered, smiling to
herself as she thought of the joke her colleagues had made. Many of
them were old enough to have been fans of Neil Diamond, and they
jokingly called her their "Sister Anne's Traveling Salvation Show." As
the primary grades mathematics specialist in the Northfield Public
Schools, Anne felt that she spent a lot of time traveling to the fourteen
K–6 schools. Today she was returning from an after-school meeting.
She wasn't sure whether she was "saving" everyone, though.

Anne walked into the main office and reached into her mailbox
for her messages. Clutching a fistful of pink and yellow message sheets,
she slowly began her ascent to the third floor. "These old buildings
are lovely with their wooden floors and Victorian architecture, but I
could do without these stairs right now," Anne thought wearily.

She arrived at her third floor office with a sigh. Her bags of resources looked at home in the room, which was cluttered with math
manipulatives, assorted textbooks and resource books, and piles of
photocopied materials for teachers. Anne looked around her office, a
former janitor's closet. "I could certainly use more space," she
thought, "but who in this building couldn't?"

Sitting at the desk wedged into one corner, Anne looked through her messages. Three teachers had called asking about getting classroom sets of counters. A principal had questions about an inservice session scheduled at his school later that week. Two teachers who had tried a lesson at Anne's suggestion had left messages, and a parent who had attended last week's family math night had given an evening phone number and asked that Anne return the call.

The shrill ring of Anne's phone interrupted her message review, and she jumped in her chair. "After all I went through to have this phone installed so I could contact people and they could call me," she thought, "why am I so easily startled every time it rings?"

"Anne, this is Vivian," the voice on the end of the line said when Anne picked up the phone. "I thought I might have missed you. Did you just get back?" Vivian Snyder was the principal of Roosevelt Elementary, where Anne had taught second-grade until three years ago, when she became the districtwide mathematics specialist for the primary grades. Vivian was no longer officially her supervisor, since Anne now reported to Claire Lindgren, the director of instruction for the district, but Anne still talked with Vivian often. She wasn't sure if it was simply because her office was here at Roosevelt or because she expected to return to full-time teaching in this building.

"I just walked in from Woodland Elementary. I was meeting after school with a group of primary teachers to talk about a training session on problem solving for their faculty," Anne replied. "What do you need?"

"How are things over at Woodland?" Vivian asked. "Do you think they're farther along than we are, here at Roosevelt, in terms of integrating more problem solving into math lessons?"

"Vivian," Anne responded, "you know how things are. Woodland is no different from any of the other elementary schools, including this one. Teachers are just in different places in terms of what they're able to do in their math classes. We're doing our best to find respectful ways to meet them where they are."

"Hmmm," Vivian murmured. She paused. "Anne, it's not only the teachers who are in different places. The parents are too. I just got a call from the superintendent. At last month's principals' meeting, a number of us were talking about the phone calls we've received and the comments we've heard from parents who think that we're no longer teaching the basics of math in our primary program."

"I've heard some of those comments from teachers as well," Anne responded.

"Well," Vivian continued, "this afternoon the superintendent got a call from a parent who is a member of the math department at the university and has a son in third grade. He was complaining that his son is not being challenged with 'hard' mathematics. The superintendent invited this guy, along with a few other parents, to the next principals' meeting to discuss the math program. I told the superintendent that you would be the ideal person to make a presentation at that meeting. You really would be great, because I know that you're trying to address some of the same concerns with the family math activities you've organized. As the elementary mathematics specialist, you could talk about the math content in our primary program and how it's connected to the NCTM standards. The catch is that the meeting is this Friday morning. Can you do it?"

Anne began to think about how she could rearrange her schedule for Friday, and opened her mouth to respond with her usual, "Yes, of course." Instead, she found she had such a rush of anger she couldn't speak. Stinging tears welled up in her eyes. For a moment, all she could do was hold the receiver and listen to Vivian asking, "Anne, are you still there?"

Anne took a deep breath and responded tersely. "Look, Vivian, I can't be a walking 'How can I help you?' math specialist any longer. I'm supposed to be at Cunningham Elementary all day on Friday doing demonstration lessons, and it's taken me a long time to set it up. Those sessions are important to me and, anyway, I think my major responsibility is to work with teachers. No one seems to understand that or think my work with teachers is a priority."

"Anne, I'm sorry you're angry, and a little surprised, too," Vivian replied. "You know I support what you're trying to do, and I didn't realize that Friday was the day that you were going to Cunningham. But I also think the superintendent's concerns about the parents are legitimate, and in your role as mathematics specialist you can best represent the district's position in implementing the recommendations in the standards."

Anne gripped the receiver more tightly. "Claire Lindgren told me that I was selected for this job because of the way I work with young kids and teachers—everyone told me that. It wasn't because of my background in math or because I might be successful working with principals or parents, especially parents who know a hundred times more math than I do. I really think my time has to be spent in classrooms with teachers and kids. That's where the real change is going to happen, and that's where I do my best work."

"You know how important it is for parents to be supportive," Vivian observed. "I mean, even something like your release time from the classroom could really be at risk if parents are complaining about where the math program is going and the school board reacts quickly."

"That's not the point, Vivian!" Anne exclaimed with a note of exasperation in her voice. "The role of the math specialist is to be with teachers and kids in the classroom! I think that explaining district decisions is the responsibility of the superintendent or Claire—or even you—but I'm being asked to do that kind of thing more and more."

"That's because it's important work," Vivian snapped. She sighed softly under her breath. "Look, the superintendent expects you to be at the meeting on Friday. What do you want to do?"

"If being the mathematics specialist means giving up my work with teachers, then I want to be back in the classroom full-time," Anne responded, unhappy with the bitterness she could hear in her voice.

There was silence on the end of the line before Vivian spoke again. "Anne, getting teachers and schools to change isn't just an educational process, it's a political process too." Vivian's voice took on a conciliatory tone. "Please at least respect the politics of all of this. In the long run, your going back to the classroom won't help the district." Anne was a good specialist, and Vivian didn't want the district to lose her, especially since she knew the district couldn't afford to find and train another teacher in this budget year.

Anne was quiet, shaken by the turn the conversation had taken and the emotions behind her response. "You'll have to let me think about this a bit. I'll call you tomorrow," she finally said.

After she had hung up the phone, Anne stared at the piles of books on her desk. What should she do? She really wanted to contribute to reform in mathematics in the district and to support other teachers. But how? And at what cost to herself?

■ ■ ■

Early Tuesday Morning

Anne called out across several cars in the parking lot of the district administration building, "Claire, do you have a minute?"

Claire Lindgren, director of instruction for the Northfield Public Schools and a friend of Anne's, turned and smiled. "I'm on my way to a meeting at one of the high schools, Anne, but I have a few minutes. What's up?"

"I need to talk to you about a conversation I had yesterday with Vivian Snyder," Anne replied, setting her bags of math materials down next to Claire's car. "I feel that things got a little out of hand, and I said some pretty strong things, and now I have to deal with it." Anne described her phone conversation with Vivian and the decision she needed to make.

After she finished, Claire patted Anne's arm sympathetically. "I'm sorry you had such a hard conversation with Vivian. I wasn't aware of the superintendent's request."

"Thanks, Claire," Anne replied, "but I need to have an answer for Vivian. That's why I want to talk to you. So tell me, what do *you* think the math specialist should be doing? Last night I looked at the original job description, but it was so general, talking about getting new ideas associated with the NCTM standards to K–3 teachers."

Claire nodded. "You're right, Anne. The description for the specialist position wasn't very specific, and that's probably an accurate reflection of where our thinking was at the time! But, getting that position posted seemed more of a formality than anything else, because we were all so clear about the need to support primary teachers, and we wanted to move quickly since we had the district funds." Claire smiled at Anne. "And you were the perfect candidate for the job! You were a veteran primary teacher with years of experience in the district. You were well liked and respected by teachers, you always went the extra mile in everything you did, and you were so good with children—and you still are all of those things. I knew at the time that mathematics wasn't necessarily your strong suit, but I also knew that we could support training for whoever was selected for the job."

"Yes, exactly!" replied Anne. "When the three of us who applied were being interviewed, the selection committee put a lot of emphasis on the ability to work with kids and teachers. I remember that, because I was so nervous about my own mathematics background and my sketchy knowledge of the NCTM standards. But, really, the job was presented as being able to work well with teachers and kids."

"Our original goals, three years ago when you were hired for this job, had to do with making teachers aware of the standards and giving them resources so they could begin to make changes in their math teaching," Claire commented. "But, we've all come to realize that changing teachers' ideas about how to teach math is much more complicated than we ever thought. It's more than getting teachers to use manipulatives. It means really helping them to understand the mathematical ideas in the curriculum. And helping principals and parents to understand them, too."

Anne nodded. "I know that there's work to do with parents. But, the work with teachers—demonstration lessons and workshops and the district math committee—that's what I see as my main responsibility. Finally, after three years, there are a lot of primary teachers who feel like they can call me and say 'I'm stuck with this and I'm not sure what to do.' I really think we're making progress." Anne drew a deep breath. "Claire, the truth is I see the parent work as part of your job, or something that the principals or the superintendent should do. I don't think it's my work. It's not about teaching and learning math in the classroom. It's not me."

Claire looked thoughtfully at Anne, and then glanced at her watch. "Oh, Anne, I'm late for that meeting! I'm sorry. I know this is an important conversation, but I have to get going and I'm booked all day. Can I catch up with you tomorrow morning so we can finish talking?"

Anne bit her lip. "I really wanted to get back to Vivian by this afternoon, because the principals' meeting is scheduled for Friday morning. Maybe I can wait until tomorrow."

She stepped back as Claire got in her car and backed out of the parking space. Picking up her bags of materials and walking slowly toward the building, Anne asked herself for what seemed like the one hundredth time, "What should the work of a math specialist be, and who defines that work? It's all so complex. But one thing I'm sure of, more primary teachers are now feeling that they have someone who is there for them, someone they can call for support. And that's important."

Facilitator's Guide

Summary of the Case

Anne Alexander, a former second-grade teacher, has been the primary grades mathematics specialist in the Northfield Public Schools for three years. She spends much of her time in the elementary schools doing demonstration lessons for teachers, developing workshops, and providing requested mathematics materials. Increasingly, Anne is involved in work with parents through family math activities and through responding to their questions about their children's mathematics program.

Anne's former principal, Vivian Snyder, relays to Anne the superintendent's request that Anne make a presentation about the content of the district math program and its connection to the NCTM standards. This presentation will be for principals and a small group of parents who have reservations about the primary grades mathematics program. Anne is reluctant to make the presentation and angry about being pulled away from what she sees as her first priority as a specialist: working with classroom teachers.

Anne's conversation with Vivian ends with Anne wondering if she should leave her position as a specialist and return to the classroom. Feeling conflicted, Anne seeks out Claire Lindgren, the district's director of instruction, to discuss the superintendent's request, Anne's challenging conversation with Vivian, and the original intent of the specialist position when it was posted three years earlier.

Claire and Anne talk about the expectations for the specialist role, particularly as it has evolved over time. But Claire needs to leave before Anne can get her views on the current specialist role or her ideas about how Anne should respond to the request from Vivian and the superintendent to make a presentation to principals and parents.

Leadership Themes

Teacher leaders are often asked to be many things to many people. The role that teacher leaders believe they "signed on" for at the outset is often different from the role they come to play over time. Situations change, new needs arise, expectations shift, and all of this affects what teacher leaders do. As the nature of their work evolves, teacher leaders find themselves interacting with other teachers, with administrators, and even with parents and community members in new ways. As a result, they need to develop effective ways to build support for themselves and their work in order to continue in what is often a challenging role.

This case provides an opportunity for discussion around

- *Negotiating new relationships:* What is the relationship between a teacher leader and his or her colleagues? How does the relationship with administrators at the building and district level change when teachers act as teacher leaders?

■ *Building support among administrators:* What kinds of support do teacher leaders need to be effective in their work? How do teacher leaders build support, particularly with administrators?

Summary of Activities

This guide offers seven sets of activities that are designed to support discussion of this case. You should feel free to add or delete activities, adapt them to suit your purposes, or rearrange the activities to fit the needs of the participants with whom you will be working. As presented here, the sets of activities are structured to focus first on the content of the case itself and then to consider larger issues beyond the immediate case scenario related to the leadership themes. Estimates of the total amount of time needed, if one were to do all the activities in a set, are indicated in parentheses below. Time estimates for individual activities are found in the descriptions that follow.

The seven sets of activities are as follows:

■ *Getting Started:* An individual written reflection and a large-group discussion of the range and variety of issues contained in the case (20–25 minutes)

■ *Understanding Perspectives:* Small- and large-group discussions to explore the perspectives represented in the case, focused specifically on the goals and the concerns of the specialist role (60–80 minutes)

■ *Creating a Job Description:* A pair activity and large-group discussion to articulate Anne's evolving responsibilities as a specialist and the expected background or expertise such a person should possess (50–70 minutes)

■ *Building Support:* A large-group discussion of the ways in which teacher leaders can build a support network to sustain their leadership work (20–30 minutes)

■ *Considering Next Steps:* Individual reflection and then pair and large-group discussions to consider the next steps Anne should take in the case (25–40 minutes)

■ *Focusing on the Teacher Leader Position in Your School or District:* A small-group activity offering the opportunity to step away from the case to list the expectations for teacher leaders in participants' sites (15–25 minutes)

■ *Wrapping Up:* Individual written reflection followed by large-group discussion to summarize insights developed about new relationships and needed support for teacher leaders (15–25 minutes)

Getting Started

These activities are meant to help participants orient themselves to the case and its story line, begin to listen to other participants' interpretations of the story, and start to track their own thinking about the case and its issues.

Individual reflection (5 minutes)

Before beginning, ask participants to write down their current ideas about what actions or next steps Anne should take and offer their reasons. Ask them to set this piece of writing aside until later in the discussion (see p. 82).

You may choose to use the following prompt:

> Before we begin to talk about the case and start to construct a shared understanding of this case and its issues, I want to take advantage of your own initial thoughts. We'll be using these ideas later in the case discussion. For now, though, write down on a piece of paper what you think Anne should do next in this situation. What response should she give to Vivian about the request to speak at the principals' meeting? Why?

Large-group discussion (15–25 minutes)

To help participants get oriented to the case, pose the following questions for discussion:

- What is this case about? What message do you take away from this case?

A question of this nature is open-ended enough that participants can respond in many ways. Encourage participants to keep their statements brief and to listen for differences among responses. Test out the ways in which you hear statements as different (e.g., "the first statement focuses on teacher leaders' expectations, while the second focuses on the goals others have for teacher leaders"). Use the statements generated to articulate the central problem(s) in the case:

- What is the central problem in this case?
- Can anyone summarize what happened in this particular case? Could anything be added to that description?

Understanding Perspectives

The characters in this case hold different views on the role of the mathematics specialist and have different kinds of relationships with one another. In order to develop more insight into each of the three main characters, this activity asks participants to analyze the goals each character has for a mathematics specialist and to reflect on the characters' relationships with one another.

Much of what makes for a rich case discussion is the analysis of the situation, the articulation of the problem(s), and the exploration of the issues. These experiences can often lead to a set of solutions that individual participants may not have imagined on first reading the case. Alternatively, the entire case experience can help participants clarify why a particular solution seems to them to be the best course of action. By writing down their solutions to this situation at the outset of the case discussion, participants are creating an artifact they can revisit at the end of the discussion.

In working with cases, particularly those with compelling story lines, participants' first reaction is to want to solve the compelling dilemma at the end of the case. The challenge for the facilitator is to keep participants on track in defining the problem and to resist the temptation to look for a solution. At this early stage of the discussion, it is more important to identify the range of issues in the case.

It's helpful to write responses on newsprint or an overhead. This way, everyone can see, avoid repeating responses, and more easily point out differences and similarities. You can then also use the list to work on the next set of questions, which focus on articulating the central problem(s).

Small-group discussion (20–30 minutes)

Ask participants to form groups of three to five people. Each small group should discuss the following questions and come to some kind of consensus that can be reported to the larger group. Encourage the groups to use evidence from the case when responding to these questions. Suggest that one person in each group act as the scribe to record responses (two to three sentences for each character).

Anne

- What goals does Anne have for herself as a mathematics specialist?
- What concerns does she have about this role?
- What adjectives might Anne use to describe her relationship to Vivian? To Claire?

Vivian

- What goals does Vivian have for the mathematics specialist?
- What concerns does she have about this role?
- What adjectives might Vivian use to describe her relationship to Anne?

Claire

- What goals does Claire have for the mathematics specialist?
- What concerns does she have about this role?
- What adjectives might Claire use to describe her relationship to Anne?

Large-group discussion (40–50 minutes)

Bring the small groups together to discuss their responses to the questions. Consider how Anne's, Vivian's, and Claire's perspectives about the specialist role are similar and different. Have each group read their responses to the questions about each character (e.g., everyone reports their responses to the questions about Anne). Then pose the following questions to the small groups:

- What ideas (about Anne or Vivian or Claire) generated the most agreement in your group?
- What ideas provoked the most disagreement?

For example, a majority of participants might see Anne as an overburdened and underappreciated specialist trying to work in classrooms with individual teachers. Others might see Claire as a director of instruction with connections to the superintendent who can help Anne work her way through her current situation. Still others might see Claire as a well-meaning but overworked district staff person who can only offer Anne moral support, given the express wishes of the superintendent and the principals.

Encourage participants to distinguish between the concerns of the characters and their own concerns. This is particularly important if participants identify with a character because they are in the same role in their own institution. The task here is to try to see the situation through the character's eyes and to use that experience to clarify which concerns can be ascribed to the character and which to the participant. Making use of the evidence in the case is one way for participants to stay true to the character's perspective.

This task and the questions that participants should consider could be listed on an overhead transparency or on newsprint, or copied for each small group.

Another option is to have participants create some kind of picture or visual representation of each character using these questions as prompts. This representation could also include references to the character's relationship to the others in the case.

After the groups have reported on their responses to the three sets of questions, discuss whether they find common ground among Vivian, Claire, and Anne in terms of their goals for the mathematics specialist role or in terms of their concerns.

■ What are some common goals Anne, Vivian, and Claire would agree on?
■ Where is their greatest divergence in terms of how they see the specialist role?

Beyond comparing the ways in which these three characters see Anne's role, go on to discuss the nature of Anne's relationship with Vivian and her relationship with Claire. When a teacher takes on the new role of teacher leader, his or her relationships with administrators and with other teachers change in ways that can be surprising to the teacher leader. The new role can raise questions about authority, accountability, and autonomy, which could result in a different kind of relationship.

Discuss the following questions:

■ What is the current relationship between Anne and Vivian? How has the relationship changed? In what ways might it still need to change?
■ What is the current relationship between Anne and Claire? How has the relationship changed? In what ways might it still need to change?

You might extend this discussion about the mathematics specialist role by adding the perspectives of characters alluded to in the case: the superintendent and the primary-grade teachers. Pose the following questions as the group considers how these perspectives inform the role of mathematics specialist:

■ When the superintendent thinks about Anne's role, what aspects are most apparent to him/her? Why?
■ When a primary-grade teacher at one of the Northfield Public Schools thinks about Anne's role, what aspects are most apparent to him or her? Why?
■ Reflect on how Anne defines her role. Is her perception of her role most similar to that of Vivian, Claire, the superintendent, or the primary-grade teachers? Why?

Creating a Job Description

In the case, Anne and Claire talk about the original mathematics specialist position posting, the job Anne applied for three years earlier. In this activity, participants will create two job descriptions for the mathematics specialist, drawing on the information in the case, their discussions about the different expectations for the role and about the different kinds of relationships the specialist will need to develop, and their own ideas, based on their own school and district experiences, about this kind of teacher leadership role. In writing the job descriptions, you may choose to have participants differentiate between the *responsibilities* of the mathematics specialist (what should he or she do?) and the *expertise or background* the applicant should bring to the job (what content, pedagogical, interpersonal, or political knowledge or skill should he or she possess?). Remind them that, as in most job postings, they are describing the ideal applicant, and it is unlikely that any one person would have all of these qualities. Considering what kind of background or expertise an applicant should have can help participants more clearly articulate the specific responsibilities of the specialist. You may also split this activity into two tasks: first, the responsibilities section of each job description and second, the desired background or expertise of the applicant. This is especially helpful if you want to elicit further discussion of the capacities an applicant is expected to bring to the specialist job.

Participants will work on two job descriptions: one, a mathematics specialist job description as it would have appeared in the Northfield Public Schools at the time Anne applied for the position three years earlier and the other, the kind of mathematics specialist job description that might be posted if Anne were to resign from the position and the district needed to hire someone else. For each job description participants should list the responsibilities of the specialist and the desired background or expertise an applicant should bring to the job.

Pair discussion (20–30 minutes)
Ask participants to work in pairs with someone they have not worked with yet. The job descriptions these pairs create can be written on newsprint and posted around the room for others to see. Ask participants to write each of them on a separate piece of paper, labeled "three years ago" and "now."

- Write a job description for the position of mathematics specialist *like Anne would have seen when she applied for the position three years ago*. In the description, focus on the responsibilities of the position and the expertise or background required of an applicant. Make the posting convey the expectations of the Northfield Public Schools at that time as clearly as possible.
- Write a job description for the position of mathematics specialist *as it would appear now, if Anne were to resign from the position and the district needed to hire someone else*. In the description, focus on the responsibilities of the position and the expertise or background required of an applicant. Make the posting convey the expectations of the Northfield Public Schools now, at the time of the case, as clearly as possible.

Participants will most likely list both serious (e.g., lead after-school workshops) and not so serious (e.g., find extra time in the day) responsibilities that teacher leaders are asked to assume. The not-so-serious responsibilities can be as revealing of the real challenges as the serious responsibilities.

In creating the earlier job description, some groups may just repeat the ideas Anne and Claire have mentioned in their conversation. Others may add to or refine these ideas to reflect the story line of the case. You should encourage participants to work from, but not limit themselves to, the specific evidence in the case.

Focusing specifically on the desired expertise or background could extend this discussion. How realistic are the expectations and what kind of person (or "superperson") is needed for this position? An extension is to rank order the kinds of experience or expertise sought. What is most important? What is nonnegotiable?

Changing the mindset that leaders act alone on behalf of others is a challenge, yet there is plenty of evidence showing that it is impossible for most people to take on and sustain the full burden of leadership by themselves, particularly when that means always having the right answers and knowing the best solution. As Palmer (1998) concludes, "The growth of any craft depends on shared practice and honest dialogue among those who do it. We grow by private trial and error, to be sure—but our willingness to try, and fail, as individuals is severely limited when we are not supported by a community that encourages such risks" (p. 144). Leaders need the support and the perspective of others in order to be effective.

Palmer goes on to talk about the importance of leaders to community: "When we talk about leadership, we have a tendency to contrast communities, which are supposed to be leaderless, with institutions, which need leaders. But it is possible to argue the opposite. Institutions can survive for a while without a leader simply by following bureaucratic rules. But community is a dynamic state of affairs that demands leadership at every turn" (p. 156). Viewing leaders as an integral part of community is quite a different mindset. (See also Lieberman and Grolnick 1999.)

Individual reflection (10 minutes)

Ask participants to post the "three years ago" job descriptions on one wall or at one end of the room and the "now" job descriptions on another wall or at the other end of the room. Have participants do a gallery walk to view these job descriptions. You may choose to read these discussion questions with participants beforehand:

- What are the similarities among the various job descriptions that Anne would have seen when she first applied for the job? Why?
- What are the similarities among the various job descriptions that reflect the position now, if Anne were to resign and the Northfield Public Schools advertised for someone else to fill that position? Why?

Large-group discussion (20–30 minutes)

After the gallery walk, briefly discuss the similarities among their "three years ago" job descriptions and the similarities among their "now" job descriptions with the group to highlight the common themes. Use these ideas to discuss the similarities *between* the two job descriptions. Focusing on job descriptions is an opportunity to consider a specialist's responsibilities and to reflect on how such a job evolves and grows over time. It's also a chance for the participants to consider whether such a job is influenced as much by the person in that position (Anne) as by those who may have hired or who work with that person (Claire, Vivian, the superintendent).

Pose the following questions:

- In what ways are the "three years ago" and "now" job descriptions similar? Why?
- How are they different?
- Why does the job description change? Whose needs or interests are represented by these changes in responsibilities or background? The teachers in the district? District administration? Parents and community? Anne?
- What experiences and expertise must an applicant bring to the job? What can be learned on the job?

The job descriptions will likely reveal a good deal about participants' own experiences with similar teacher leader positions. In asking participants to discuss which of the posted job descriptions would be more appealing to them, you are guiding them to discuss the responsibilities they could see themselves assuming. Their capacity to imagine themselves in a role like this is both a statement of what they think a teacher leader *should* do and what they as teacher leaders believe they are *able* to do. Consider the following question for discussion:

- Which job description, "three years ago" or "now," would be more appealing to you? Which one might you apply for? Why?

Building Support

Most specialists cannot carry out their role in isolation. Many teacher leaders burn out if they persist in believing that they, and they alone, bear full responsibility for this leadership work. This set of questions invites participants to consider how a specialist such as Anne might build support among her colleagues that can help her be more successful in her role.

Large-group discussion (20–30 minutes)

This discussion should build on ideas developed in earlier activities about the nature of Anne's role as a specialist and her relationships with people like Vivian and Claire. It is intended to encourage participants to think creatively and concretely about how a teacher leader might get other people to join in leadership work and thus build more support to sustain the work. A support network like this might include colleagues who share similar leadership positions, "superiors" in the district administration, fellow teachers, principals, and community members.

Pose the following questions for discussion:

- If Anne were trying to build support among people who could join her in some way in the work of a mathematics specialist, who might be part of Anne's support network?
- Identify two strategies Anne could use to elicit support from others, especially support that is more than offering encouragement from the sidelines.
- Remember that support is a two-way street—it's both about the support that Anne needs from others and the support that she can offer them in return. Focus on two characters, Vivian and Claire. What support might Anne receive from and give to each of them?

Considering Next Steps

Many participants expect that problem solving is the most important, or even the only, activity for a case discussion. At this point, after participants have considered various perspectives, written job descriptions, and/or strategized about building support for the specialist, return to the question of what Anne might do next in the situation described in the case.

Individual reflection (5–10 minutes)

Ask participants to reflect on their thinking at the start of the case discussion (see p. 77), about what Anne should do next in this case. You might want participants to reread the last page of the case to remind themselves of the situation as the case ends:

- Find the paper on which you recorded your initial ideas about what Anne should do next in this case. Read it over and now add, amend, or affirm your response.

A teacher leader like Anne could build support among colleagues through a variety of methods.

- *Ask for help ("Help me figure out what to do here").*
- *Delegate tasks ("I would like you to do this").*
- *Enlarge the capacity of others to do certain things that the leader currently does ("Let me help you figure out how to do this").*
- *Secure resources ("Each grade level should have a set of manipulatives in the building so that I don't have transport them around the district").*
- *Seek out people who can provide moral support ("Remind me of why I'm doing this work").*

These questions might also be used in individual written reflection, as another small-group activity, or as an assignment to do outside the case discussion.

Pair discussion (10–15 minutes)

Ask participants to pair up with another person and share their ideas about Anne's next steps.

■ How are each of your suggestions for Anne's next step similar or different? Why?

■ Did your suggestions change in any way over the course of the case discussion? If so, explain what led to the change. What other ideas or perspectives informed your revision? If your suggested next step remained the same, explain what you heard or considered during the discussion that confirmed your original idea.

Large-group discussion (10–15 minutes)

Bring the pairs together into the larger group. Ask participants to talk about suggestions that were different from their original thinking. Generate a list of insights or ideas that were most powerful in reshaping views on how Anne should proceed.

Focusing on the Teacher Leader Position in Your School or District

This activity uses the ideas participants have considered earlier in the case discussion and applies it to the current or anticipated leadership role of specialist in their school or district. It is easy to miss the connections between the case and one's own situation ("we don't have release time for our specialists" or "our teacher leaders are in science, not mathematics"), and you may need to encourage participants to focus on how the role of specialist, or an equivalent teacher leader position, is framed in their school or district. Ask them to pay attention to the relationships that exist, or need to be developed, between the teacher leader and others, and to the kinds of support the teacher leader could develop to be successful in this role.

Small-group discussion (15–25 minutes)

Have participants form small groups. If there are natural groups (teachers from the same school, educators from the same district), this is a good time for those groups to work together. Describe or post the following tasks for small groups to discuss and then record.

■ List the responsibilities a specialist in your school or district currently has or would have. (If there is no such position, imagine that you are writing the job description for such a position.) Which responsibilities do you see as most important? Why?

■ List the kinds of experience or expertise that someone in this position would need. You might describe the experience or expertise of someone currently in that position or the experience or expertise someone should have to be successful. Which kinds of experience or expertise do you see as most important? Why?

In this activity, participants may each record their ideas, or put together one set of responses representing the group's collective thinking. This activity can be extended in a large-group discussion or by copying and distributing responses after the discussion. It can also serve as a bridge into a follow-up discussion or professional development experience.

- Identify two or three other people in your school or district who might come up with a similar list of responsibilities and experiences for a specialist. Why might their lists be similar to yours? Also identify two or three others in your school or district whose lists would be different and consider why their lists would be different. Where is the common ground between your list and theirs?
- Identify two or three people who should be part of any support network for a specialist in your school or district. What kind of support can they offer? Why might they offer this support?

Wrapping Up

This closing activity is designed to help participants arrive at some closure to their work with the case. Adapt the activity to fit the case experience you have constructed with participants. How you wrap up the case discussion and what you emphasize will depend on the purpose you have identified for this case experience.

Individual reflection (5–10 minutes)

Ask participants to review the various parts of the case experience by referring to their notes, to the newsprint and transparency lists, and to other artifacts from the discussion in order to write down reflections on one or both of the following questions:

- When teachers act as teacher leaders, in what ways do their relationships with colleagues and administrators change?
- What are the various kinds of support teacher leaders need to be effective in their roles?

Large-group discussion (10–15 minutes)

Ask participants to share their reflections. Point out similarities among responses to help them summarize insights developed from the case discussion. If you have asked participants to reflect on both questions, be sure to allocate time to talk about both responses.

CHAPTER 5

Who's the Expert Around Here?

Case

Paula Winslow, *Mathematics specialist and first-grade teacher*
Jackie Randolph, *Third-grade teacher*
Gail Coombs, *Third-grade teacher*
Bob Rollins, *K–12 mathematics coordinator*
Zoe Sansarian, *Mathematics specialist*
Delores Dandridge, *Mathematics specialist*
Faith Smith, *Mathematics specialist*

Wednesday Morning, 8:05

"Oh, hello, Jackie! I was just dropping off the new set of tangrams* I ordered for you." Paula Winslow, a mathematics specialist, greeted Jackie Randolph as they met in the long hallway outside Jackie's classroom. "I left them on your desk with a note. If you want me to come to your class to do some demonstration lessons using them, I could certainly do that. Okay?"

Jackie looked startled. "Well, it depends on whether I can find the place and time in my lessons," she replied slowly, avoiding Paula's eyes. "Thanks for bringing them by, Paula."

"No problem," responded Paula. "Gail told me last week that you had talked about trying tangrams after our last inservice session on math manipulatives, so I thought I would just go ahead and bring these to you."

---

*A tangram is a square cut into seven pieces, which can be rearranged into many other shapes to explore area, congruence, fractions, etc.

Jackie's face tightened. "Oh, I see," she said. She glanced into her room. "You'll have to excuse me, Paula. There's only a few minutes before the morning bell and I have some things to do before the kids get here. Wednesday mornings are really busy in my room."

Paula nodded. "Sure. I have to get back to my classroom, too. I'll see you later." She walked quickly down the hall.

Arms folded across her chest, Jackie turned and saw Gail Coombs hurrying toward her from the opposite direction. Like Jackie, Gail was a third-grade teacher and had the room next to her.

"Morning, Jackie!" Gail called. "Was that Paula Winslow you were talking with? I haven't seen her on this side of the building for a while."

"Yes, it was," Jackie replied curtly as she followed Gail into her classroom. "Paula came by my room this morning to drop off some tangrams and invited herself into my classroom to do some kind of demonstration lesson with them. She said you told her I was interested in trying the tangrams out. Is that true?"

Surprised, Gail looked at Jackie with wide eyes. "Yes, it's true. I mean, you did tell me after the last district math inservice that the tangram lesson made an impression and you wanted to try them in your own classroom. Maybe a day or so later, I was walking into the building with Paula, and she asked me how I had liked the inservice session. I told her I thought it was pretty good, overall, and I shared your comment. I was just making conversation, really. Why? What's the problem?"

"I don't like feeling pressured to make changes in my teaching, and that is exactly how I felt this morning when Paula arrived with the tangrams," Jackie retorted angrily. She took a deep breath and continued, "Look, I don't blame you for Paula's visit. It's just that, like I've said before, I need to go at my own pace. I did enjoy seeing their demonstration at the inservice. I admit I've had some difficulty in making sense of what the textbook is doing with geometry in third grade. The transition from being a fifth-grade teacher is more difficult than I thought." Jackie paused. "I realize I don't know everything I need to know about third grade, but this is just my second year at it. Besides, we don't get to geometry until the end of the year. I can't even think about it now."

Gail smiled. "I think we're all having some problems this year with this new math curriculum we have. I mean, I'm trying to emphasize problem solving in my math class, but I have no idea how to make some of the changes that Paula has described in some of her meetings with us."

After a moment's hesitation, Jackie asked, "What exactly is Paula supposed to be doing anyway? I mean, I don't think I've ever been totally clear about the math specialist role."

"Well," replied Gail, "Paula is still teaching her first-grade class, but she's also supposed to be an additional resource for teachers in math, especially K–3 teachers. I think the specialists are also supposed to do some things around family math programs and coordinate new math materials, making them available to teachers. But other people might have a different impression of what they do."

As the bell rang and the sound of feet and excited voices filled the hallway, Jackie gave Gail a long look as they walked toward the doorway. "So, do you think Paula is the expert at mathematics in this building?"

Gail stopped and turned toward Jackie. "I don't know," she replied, over the heads of the children hurrying into the classroom. "I do know that because of the professional development she has been involved with she certainly knows more than I do about the standards and what seems to be changing in math."

■ ■ ■

Saturday Morning, 9:35

Paula Winslow raced through the doorway of the elementary school media center, wondering if she would be late for the round-robin updates. She counted on hearing from the other nine mathematics specialists to get some ideas to bring back to her building. Paula slid into the remaining open seat at the table just as Bob Rollins, the K–12 math coordinator, whistled—his personal signal for starting meetings. The conversations gradually ended as people turned their attention to Bob. "Everyone is here, and that's great!" he exclaimed warmly. "So, let's get caught up with one another. What's happening with you? How are things going?"

For a few moments the group fell silent. Bob rolled his eyes in amazement. "I've made this group speechless. I can't believe it!" he said. Everyone laughed.

Zoe Sansarian spoke up. "Our K–3 math group is really following through on our plans for a buildingwide math Olympics. We've had two meetings. Both of them included a number of the fourth- through sixth-grade teachers, and you've heard me talk about how tough it's been to get them involved. The last meeting included two parent representatives, so I am feeling pretty positive about that."

"Zoe," asked Delores Dandridge, "what is the level of participation among the teachers? Do you think it's really going to be a buildingwide event? Is everyone as enthusiastic as you are?"

"Well," Zoe replied, "the teachers in my building are as enthusiastic as they are going to get. At least I have a teacher representative from each grade and our principal has been really supportive. So, yeah, it's going to be okay."

"Speaking of enthusiasm," Paula remarked, "I'm still struggling with how to get into some of the classrooms to do demonstration lessons. You know, Bob, the kind of thing you've been encouraging us to do as a follow-up to the district inservices on the math manipulatives. Boy, it's rough. And I'm not sure I like that role, anyway."

"What do you mean, Paula?" Bob asked.

Paula took a deep breath. "I guess it's being seen as the expert at something when I certainly don't consider myself the expert. But when I suggest that I visit someone's classroom to do a demonstration lesson, that's how I think I'm being perceived. And I'm not comfortable with it at all."

Delores caught her eye and replied, "Paula, I'm so relieved you said that about the demonstration lessons. I wanted to bring it up last month, but chickened out. Everyone seemed so upbeat about how things were going."

"My school is such a mixed bag," Paula continued. "I mean, some of the teachers seem really okay with the math specialist thing. I did a demonstration lesson with one of the first-grade teachers last week and I thought it went well. But there are other teachers in the building who make it very clear that they don't want me in their classrooms at all."

Paula paused, about to describe her encounter with Jackie Randolph, when Zoe spoke up. "Yes, it's like walking on a crate of eggs. You don't want to be offensive or seem as if you think you know it all, so you say things like, 'I know you probably know how to do this, but since you haven't done it before, would you like me to go over some of the ways I do it?' And when it's an older, more experienced teacher, that can be awkward."

The room fell silent for a moment until Paula spoke again. "I've never been comfortable with the part of our role that makes us look as if we're better than other teachers—that expert thing. Maybe I'm overreacting, but some days I almost think we're seen more as administrators than as teachers. I can see being a resource to teachers if they come to us, but beyond that, I don't know."

"Paula," Bob responded, "I don't think we ever intended specialists to be seen as experts. My expectation is that you will be a resource to your schools, coordinating math materials, establishing a districtwide family math program, trying to get teachers more familiar with the NCTM Standards documents, and providing some leadership to help schools take more responsibility for their own math inservice activities as needs arise. I thought the demonstration lesson idea was generated in this group when some of you saw some math teaching in your buildings that you were uncomfortable with. Is my memory off the mark here?"

Paula sighed. "No, Bob, it's not, but I don't think we've ever talked about some of our experiences trying to work in another teacher's classroom. It may seem simple, but it's not."

"You know," Delores commented, "I only go into the classrooms of the teachers who want me there. That way there is no hostility."

"How many of you have been struggling with being seen as an expert, especially around something like demonstration lessons?" Bob asked the group. Seven of the ten raised their hands. "Okay, that's a lot of discomfort. I guess when I'm in your schools, talking to you and talking with the other teachers, I just haven't picked up on this issue." He thought for a moment and then leaned forward in his chair. "I wonder if the expectations for the specialist's role have changed over time. When we started a year and half ago, we were just trying to get everyone to be more aware of the changes going on in mathematics, like the standards and the new curriculum materials, the need to stress something else besides worksheets. But now, as we're implementing the new elementary math curriculum, you are all leaders who are capable of modeling a different kind of math instruction. I know it may not be comfortable for you but, to be perfectly honest, I'm not sure we are going to change anything unless we can get teachers to be more reflective about their teaching, and sometimes that means you have to challenge them to grow. I am convinced that teachers teaching other teachers is a powerful way to change schools. I think that means that you all have to be more proactive and take the first steps to help others teach math differently."

Paula interjected, "Bob, I'm not even talking about teaching. I'm talking about attitudes some teachers have, the ones who are the hold-outs, who won't even begin to think about how they might make changes in their math teaching and who make it difficult for the teachers who do. For example, one of the teachers in my building confides to parents who have questions about the math program that she doesn't agree with the way math is being taught in our school now either. That really makes it tough for those of us who are trying to teach in new ways."

"Paula," Faith Smith spoke in a quiet voice, "I think we simply have to ignore those attitudes. We just have to concentrate on finding ways to empower the teachers who want to make changes. I mean, no one is going to change because we say they should. But those teachers who want to change need ideas and support."

Zoe added, "I think the way I can best help people who want to change is by concentrating on activities that are outside the classroom, not inside. I don't want to interfere with other people's teaching decisions, even if I don't agree with what they're doing. Who am I to tell them that they should change or what they should do differently?" Zoe paused as several others nodded. She turned to Bob as she continued, "You know, Bob, it just struck me why I have been so uncomfortable with our math specialist title. It's too formal. It sets us apart from other teachers even though we are still teachers. Teaching is our primary job. I guess I don't feel prepared for taking on that kind of leadership, and I'm not sure it's appreciated anyway."

Faith shook her head. "I see this leadership question differently. I think we did sign on for leadership responsibilities. I think whether we are a resource for teaching materials, for questions about math content, or for family math programs, we are providing leadership. We each just do it differently, according to our different schools and different situations."

Except for the whirring sound of the overhead fans, the room was silent. Paula looked around the table and saw that some of the other specialists were nodding in agreement with what Faith had said, while others sat with blank expressions and one or two with furrowed brows as they pondered her comments. Bob's usually cheerful face looked distressed.

Bob laughed weakly, "Well, I guess this isn't the best time to mention that I want you all to work more with the second-grade teachers, most of whom are feeling kind of panicked over the state-mandated math tests at grade two, is it?"

Paula opened her mouth to respond, and then shut it quickly. She thought to herself, "I've already said too much, but it's what I really feel! We're still getting resistance from teachers who don't want our help using things like manipulatives. How can Bob expect us to work with all the second-grade teachers on a high-stakes issue like the state test? Besides, that will really make us look like we're the ones with all the answers—and we're not!"

Facilitator's Guide

Summary of the Case

Paula Winslow is the mathematics specialist for her building, in addition to her role as a full-time, first-grade teacher. In her specialist role, Paula helps teachers secure and use mathematics materials, builds awareness of the NCTM standards, gives after-school workshops for teachers, and offers demonstration lessons. The case opens as Paula is delivering some mathematics materials to Jackie Randolph, a teacher in her school. Jackie's reluctance to talk with Paula about the use of the materials or invite Paula into her classroom leads both to reflect independently about the appropriate role of the mathematics specialist.

The case continues when Paula takes up this issue with the other mathematics specialists and with Bob Rollins, the district mathematics coordinator, at their regular meeting. There, she talks about the resistance she is facing from some teachers in her school, as well as her own reluctance to present herself as an expert among her colleagues.

A discussion among the specialists about the difficulties of inviting oneself into another teacher's classroom to do a demonstration lesson ignites a revealing conversation about the specialists' different views about their role. Various specialists talk about their expectations and those of the teachers at their schools as well as the challenges they each face in their work. Paula continues to raise her own concerns about the specialist role, which are heightened when Bob Rollins suggests that they add a new challenge to their work responsibilities.

Leadership Themes

Acting in a leadership role invariably raises questions, for the teacher leader and for his or her colleagues, about what constitutes appropriate behavior. Frequently, as in this case, questions about the leadership role are tied up with the issue of expertise. The expertise issue is given even greater attention when, as seen in this case, the teacher leader remains a full-time classroom teacher.

This case provides an opportunity for discussions around

- *Developing expertise:* What is the nature of the expertise needed by teacher leaders? For what tasks? In what settings? When should that expertise be developed?

- *Dealing with resistant colleagues:* How can teacher leaders interpret the resistance they perceive in their colleagues? How can they respond to this resistance?

Summary of Activities

This guide offers six sets of suggested activities designed to support discussion of this case. You should feel free to add or delete activities, adapt them to suit your purposes, or rearrange them to fit the needs of the group with which you will be working. As presented here, the sets of activities are structured to focus first on the content of the case itself and then to consider larger issues related to the leadership themes beyond the immediate case scenario. Estimates of the total amount of time needed, if one were to do all of the activities in a set, are given in parentheses. Time estimates for individual activities are given in the descriptions that follow.

The six sets of activities are as follows:

- *Getting Started:* A large-group discussion of the range and variety of issues contained in the case (15–20 minutes)
- *Understanding Perspectives:* Two rounds of small- and large-group discussions to explore perspectives represented by the various characters in the case, focusing specifically on the characters' different expectations for the mathematics specialist (65–90 minutes)
- *Decoding Expertise:* A sequence of small-group discussion, silent reflection, large-group discussion, small-group discussion, and individual written reflection to investigate different dimensions of expertise for teacher leaders (100–145 minutes)
- *Figuring Out the Timing:* A debate format focusing on whether expertise is something that a teacher leader must possess before starting leadership work or can develop during the course of leadership work (30–40 minutes)
- *Working with Resistant Colleagues:* A large-group discussion followed by a pair activity on the meaning of some teachers' resistance to the efforts of teacher leaders (50–80 minutes)
- *Wrapping Up:* A small- and large-group discussion of the next steps that Paula, Bob, and others might take in the case (30–45 minutes)

Getting Started

This set of questions is meant to help participants orient themselves to the case and its story line, begin to listen to the other participants' interpretations of the story, and identify central problems around which to focus subsequent activities.

Large-group discussion (15–20 minutes)

Begin the discussion by asking for summaries of the case to clarify the chronology, the important details, and the cast of characters. Then ask participants to identify what they see as the central problem. Expect that participants will identify several different problems. The object at this point in the discussion is not to settle on one problem as definitive but to consider the range of problems participants have identified. Discuss the issues that seem to contribute to the various problems. In view of your purpose for the case experience and the kinds of activities

Depending on the size of the group, you might choose to divide the participants into smaller discussion groups. If possible, have a knowledgeable facilitator within each of the small groups, or instruct a participant to play this role, so that these initial discussions stay focused on identifying the problems within the case. Facilitators in each small group should help participants come to agreement about the broad outlines of the case and the kinds of issues it raises. If this discussion takes place within small groups, be sure to provide an opportunity for each group to report back, ensuring that everyone (including you) has a sense of what the whole group is thinking.

you have selected, indicate which problem(s) subsequent discussion
and work will highlight.

Some useful discussion questions are

- Can someone summarize what happened in this particular case?
  What could be added to that description?
- What is the central problem in this case?
- Are there other dilemmas? What are they?
- What do you believe are the issues that contributed to these
  problems?

Understanding Perspectives

This case explores a particular teacher leader role, that of the specialist
in mathematics, from the point of view of different characters: various
mathematics specialists, classroom teachers, and a district mathematics coordinator. As the case unfolds, we hear the characters' questions
and concerns about the nature of the work of the mathematics specialist, the expected expertise the specialist should have, and the challenges of working with colleagues within their school. The activities in
this section help participants to investigate the perspectives of different characters in order to develop a deeper understanding of this
teacher leader role.

Small-group discussion (15–20 minutes)

This discussion begins by considering four characters' points of view
on the mathematics specialist role. Ask participants to form small
groups based on their choice of (or assignment to) one of the following
characters in the case: Jackie Randolph, Zoe Sansarian, Faith Smith, or
Bob Rollins. A later activity asks participants to focus directly on Paula
Winslow's perspective. However, attending to the diverse perspectives of these four characters first will enrich the discussion of Paula's
perspective.

Read or post the following questions for all small groups:

- What is this character's view of the mathematics specialist role?
  Identify three or four phrases this character might use to describe
  the role of the mathematics specialist.
- What are this character's concerns about how the role is currently
  being carried out?
- Select a quote from the case (one sentence or less) that best illustrates the perspective of this character on the mathematics specialist role.

Large-group discussion (20–30 minutes)

Drawing on the small-group, conversations, ask all participants to list
phrases that describe the role of the mathematics specialist from the
perspective of their character and invite the rest to indicate whether

their character would agree or disagree with the phrase as an accurate description. All groups will not agree. For some characters, particular phrases will not apply at all. For some groups, however, these same phrases will seem to be ideal descriptors of the mathematics specialist role. Writing these phrases on newsprint or an overhead will make it easier to add to the list and to use the list for the next small-group discussion.

Ask the groups to cite evidence from the case to back up their choice of phrases. The purpose of this activity is to help participants explore the perspectives of different characters toward the specialist role and, more important, why they hold that view. The discussion can then be extended to explore the values or expectations of participants about the work of such teacher leaders.

Pose the following questions:

- As (name of particular character), what phrases did you come up with to describe the role of mathematics specialist?
- Which other characters agree with that phrase? Why?
- What evidence from the case can help us understand why that particular phrase represents your character's perspective on the specialist role?

In addition, ask groups to reflect on how their character's concerns colored his or her perspective on the mathematics specialist role. You might use the following questions:

- What were your character's concerns about the mathematics specialist role? Why?
- How did those concerns shape his or her expectations of what mathematics specialists should do?

Small-group discussion (15–20 minutes)

In the same small groups as before, participants can discuss how Paula views her role as a mathematics specialist. Encourage participants to draw on the earlier list of phrases compiled by the larger group.

- What are Paula's concerns about the mathematics specialist role at this time? Why?
- How would you characterize Paula's view of the specialist role? What phrases could you use?
- Select a quote from the case (one sentence or less) that best illustrates Paula's perspective.

Large-group discussion (15–20 minutes)

In the larger group, discuss the additional ideas that have emerged from the examination of Paula's perspective on the mathematics specialist role. Explore the ways in which each small group views Paula.

The group that discussed Bob's views, for example, might note that "as Bob, we feel that the mathematics specialist should be proactive and reach out to other teachers." Ask this group to cite evidence from the text to back up their claim. Those who discussed Zoe's view might agree with the adjective "proactive," interpreting Zoe's comment about "concentrating on activities that are outside the classroom" as an example of being proactive. Discussing where and how Bob would want the specialists to be proactive, compared to Zoe's view, would be a helpful way to explore what this adjective means and would shed light on each character's perspectives on the mathematics specialist role.

Each small group could record their responses on newsprint and display them for others to see. For example, each group might list the phrases they believe Paula would use to describe her role as a mathematics specialist, along with the quote they believe best illustrates her perspective.

Are they all in agreement? What ideas have prompted different points of view? The purpose of this discussion is to create a deeper under-standing of the mathematics specialist role by considering Paula's perspective in comparison with those of the other characters (Bob, Zoe, Faith, and Jackie).

■ What phrases would Paula use to describe her specialist role?
■ In what ways is Paula's perspective on the mathematics specialist role similar to that of Zoe? of Bob? of Faith? of Jackie?
■ What is "special" about the "specialist" role? In what ways has Paula "specialized"?

Decoding Expertise

Many teacher leaders are concerned about whether they have suffi-cient expertise to be successful in their role. In the case, we heard the concerns of Paula and her colleagues about their own expertise as mathematics specialists. However, what each character means by "ex-pertise" and what participants in the case discussion mean are likely to be different. This activity gives participants the chance to decode or deconstruct expertise and to consider what issues are bound up in the image of teacher leader as expert. This activity highlights two issues: knowledge and status. By *knowledge*, we mean what it is that a teacher leader knows or should know to be effective: content, pedagogy, larger reforms, and professional development with adults. By *status*, we mean the often untested assumption that being an expert means setting oneself up as superior to others ("I know more than you do") or as an authority ("I'm in the position to tell you what to do").

Small-group discussion (20–30 minutes)

Introduce the discussion questions by describing the different kinds of knowledge (of subject matter, pedagogy, reform, and professional development) one might expect a teacher leader to possess. Alterna-tively, you could generate a list with the participants that might be similar to or different from this list.

Ask participants to form small groups, different from those in earlier activities, of four to five people each. The discussion task is to define what each kind of knowledge means in the context of this case and to offer an example from the case that discusses or hints at that particular kind of knowledge expertise. You can use the list below or develop one of your own. The purpose is to distinguish among the different kinds of knowledge teacher leaders might need and to apply those ideas to this case (and in other situations). In this way, partici-pants begin to clarify the question "Who's the expert?" and increase the likelihood that they can answer it satisfactorily.

Knowledge is a major component of teacher leader expertise—but there are many kinds of knowledge. At the end of the first scene,

Jackie asks the question, "Do you think Paula is the expert at mathematics in this building?" Paraphrasing that question, pose the following questions about the types of knowledge a teacher leader might need:

- Subject matter knowledge (Am I the *mathematics* expert around here?)
- Pedagogy knowledge (Am I the *teaching* expert around here?)
- Reform knowledge (Am I the *change* expert around here?)
- Professional development knowledge (Am I the *adult learning* expert around here?)

Set the following tasks for small groups, asking them to create some written record of their ideas by the end of the discussion:

- Define what you believe is meant by each of type of expert knowledge in the context of this case.
- Identify an example from the case in which that particular kind of expert knowledge is discussed or hinted at.

Large-group discussion (15–20 minutes)

Ask a representative from each small group to report on one kind of expert knowledge, referring to the written record from the small-group discussion. Ask other participants to comment on whether the definition of, for example, subject matter knowledge presented was similar to or different from the one they developed in their own small groups. Encourage participants to cite an example from the case to ground the discussion about particular kinds of expert knowledge. Continue until ideas about each kind of knowledge have been presented to the larger group. Recording this information on an overhead projector or newsprint is important in order to refer to these ideas in the subsequent discussion about expert status.

Silent reflection (5–10 minutes)

In the larger group, ask participants to reflect on the status issues implicit in teacher leadership expertise. For many teacher leaders, expertise is something that sets them apart from their teacher colleagues. Teachers who believe the teaching profession to be egalitarian—premised on equality among teachers—may find the idea of a teacher *leader* contradictory. Expertise is often the factor that sets teacher leaders apart from—and, some would claim, over—their colleagues.

Use the following prompts for silent reflection. You can read them aloud, put them on an overhead projector, direct participants' attention to the particular quotes in the case text, or make copies of the quotes or the entire task for individuals.

Reflect on the following quotes from the case. How is expertise for these characters tied up with status issues—how they believe their colleagues view them as mathematics specialists?

Some participants will expect teacher leaders to be subject matter specialists who have a deep understanding of their discipline and can apply that knowledge to their leadership work. Others will assume that teacher leaders bring other kinds of knowledge to their work and that even if their subject matter knowledge is not so extensive, they can still be effective. Successful classroom teaching is increasingly linked to the teacher's subject area knowledge (Darling-Hammond, Ball 1998). The same claim can be made for teacher leadership, but raises questions that merit discussion:

- *How deep should one's subject matter knowledge be? Is deeper always better?*
- *Is breadth of knowledge, across a domain like mathematics for example, similarly important?*
- *To what extent is one's subject matter knowledge developed outside one's teacher leadership work? Through one's teacher leadership work?*
- *How much teacher leader expertise is based on subject matter knowledge?*

Similar questions could be posed to consider other kinds of expert knowledge.

- Zoe: "You know, Bob, it just struck me why I have been so uncomfortable with our math specialist title. It's too formal. It sets us apart from other teachers even though we are still teachers."
- Paula: "I've never been comfortable with the part of our role that makes us look as if we're better than other teachers—that expert thing. Maybe I'm overreacting, but some days I almost think we're seen more as administrators than as teachers."

Large-group discussion (30–40 minutes)

After individuals have had an opportunity to reflect on these quotes and on their ideas about the status expertise does or does not confer upon teacher leaders, bring the group together for a large-group discussion. Listen for ways in which participants interpret the quotes and the inherent status issues: superior to another ("I know more than you do"), authority over another ("I'm in the position to tell you what to do"), or different from another ("I've been singled out"). Be attentive to the other roles to which the specialist's role is compared, such as administrator, master teacher, or mentor. Be alert to the comparisons made with teacher leaders, especially those that don't always have positive connotations, such as "goody two-shoes," "little Miss Helpful," or principal's/supervisor's "right-hand man."

Consider the following questions:

- What do you think Zoe meant when she said that the specialist title "sets us apart"? In what ways?
- Why was Paula concerned with the "part of our role that makes us look . . . better than other teachers"?
- What expertise might Zoe or Paula have that would put them in a different or special relationship with their colleagues? Should it put them in a different relationship?
- Aside from a role like mathematics specialist, are there other ways in which teachers already differentiate themselves in their relationships with one another? What are these based on? Should there be differences in teachers' relationships with one another?

Add to the discussion by drawing on ideas about expert knowledge developed earlier. Refer to the public record of the previous large-group discussion. Pose the following questions:

- What kind of knowledge (content, pedagogy, reform, professional development) seems most likely to set mathematics specialists apart from their colleagues? Why?
- What kind of knowledge is most "specialized" for a mathematics specialist? Is this knowledge likely or unlikely to set a specialist apart from colleagues?

Small-group discussion (20–30 minutes)

This activity can conclude your inquiry into expertise. It offers participants the opportunity to articulate the kind of expertise called for in various situations in the case, as well as in their own situations outside the case. Ask participants to return to the small groups of the earlier discussion of expert knowledge to consider the issues of knowledge and implied status.

Make the following questions available to participants by posting them on newsprint or on an overhead or by making copies for each small group:

- What expertise do the following situations require?

    Doing a demonstration lesson, such as Paula did with a first-grade teacher in her building.

    Organizing a buildingwide math Olympics, such as Zoe was doing at her school.

    Supporting second-grade teachers as they prepare their students for the state-mandated test, as Bob suggested.

- What expertise do you think the following situations would require?

    Leading workshops for colleagues at a different grade level, for example, a primary (K–3) teacher working with intermediary (grades 4–6) colleagues or a middle school teacher working with elementary school colleagues.

    Advocating for mathematics education reform on a site-based council, consisting of teachers, administrators, and parents.

- What situations in your own school or district call upon teacher leader expertise? What kind of expertise?

Individual written reflection (10–15 minutes)

This activity might be used to extend your inquiry about expertise in teacher leadership. It gives participants the chance to collect their thoughts and reflect on what they have discussed and encourages them to synthesize the ideas to apply to their own situations. Writing ideas down rather than only thinking about them makes this experience more tangible for participants and gives them a record of what they were thinking about at this point in the case experience.

Choose among questions like the following:

- Which expertise issues strike you as most difficult to resolve: knowledge or status? Why?
- What do you think Paula might need to do, consider, or learn to resolve her concerns about her own expertise?
- In terms of his or her concerns about expertise, which character felt most familiar to you? Why?

These questions are prompts for reflection, and you should choose only a couple for participants to focus on as they write. You might like to substitute other questions that are specific to the group's school or district situations. Have participants seek out a comfortable place for their reflection and writing. This activity might also serve as an outside assignment and could act as a bridge between discussions of this case and other cases.

*Of interest here is research sup-
porting the idea that teachers'
professional expertise necessarily
develops over time. Webb, Heck,
and Tate (1996) identify seven
elements that promote professional growth: disequilibrium,
exposure to new ideas, belief in
the positive effect of those new
ideas on students' learning, access
to modeling of good teaching,
support for one's own change,
individual experimentation, and
individual and collaborative reflection with colleagues.*

*Debating two different positions
about timing can extend the previous discussions about expert
knowledge and expert status.
Alternatively, you might use the
debate format to help participants
collect and sort out ideas about
expertise if you have not already
discussed this issue extensively.
The amount of structure you offer
will depend on how much time
and energy participants have put
into investigating these issues up
to this point.*

*You could divide the large
group into two, with each representing one position. Or you
might divide the group into
smaller groups, pairing up two
small groups where each small
group articulates one position.
You would then have multiple
debates going on, without any
attempt to have everyone hear all
the arguments.*

*You might also choose to be
more faithful to general debating
rules by allowing time for rebut-
tals or questions.*

■ In your school or district, what strategies have you used or observed that you believe were effective in addressing concerns
about expertise? Why were these strategies effective?

Figuring Out the Timing

Questions about expertise are often linked to concerns about timing:
When should expert knowledge be acquired? Is expert status assigned
or is it earned? Whether expertise should be a prerequisite for teacher
leadership work or understood as an outcome of teacher leadership
work, both views reveal deeply held ideas about the necessary knowledge one needs or the status one should claim in order to be a successful teacher leader. This activity helps participants integrate their
earlier reflections on expertise and apply them to the question of timing: At what point in their prior experiences, preparation, or leadership work should teacher leaders be expected to have acquired the
appropriate expertise?

Debate (30–40 minutes)

Some believe that teacher leaders should bring expertise to their role
(that is, they are chosen because they have certain expertise or receive
training to develop particular expertise before they work with their
colleagues). Others believe that teacher leaders develop expertise as
they carry out this role (that is, teacher leaders become more knowledgeable as they teach or share ideas with others or they become better able to identify areas where they want to extend their knowledge
because of their work with colleagues). These contrasting positions
have implications for recruiting, training, supporting, and "marketing" teacher leaders, and they can send very different messages about
teacher leaders' status and knowledge.

A debate can be a hotly contested argument or a deliberate consideration of different points of view. Either form is possible, depending
on the temperament of the group and your own interests as the facilitator. The value of the debate format is that it reveals the assumptions
and ideas underlying each position or resolution. The purpose here is
less to convince others of a particular point of view than to gather,
synthesize, and articulate ideas expressing a particular position.

The two positions for the debate are

1. Resolved: Expertise is a prerequisite for effective teacher leadership.
2. Resolved: Expertise is an outcome of effective teacher leadership.

Once the groups have been assembled, give each some time to
discuss the resolution and organize points related to its position. The
merit of this activity arises from the ways in which participants articulate their ideas, so allow enough time for this work to occur. Then,
arrange for the two groups to present their positions to one another.

You might act as a timekeeper or appoint someone else to keep time, allowing no more than five minutes for each position.

Working with Resistant Colleagues

In this case, Paula and the other mathematics specialists raise concerns about the resistance that they are facing from their colleagues, particularly when they go into colleagues' classrooms or focus on classroom instruction strategies. The first scene, with Paula and Jackie and then with Jackie and Gail, is a prime example of these concerns for Paula. This scene also offers the chance to explore Jackie's concerns and questions. Resistance, then, can be explored from two perspectives: from Paula's perspective, as the one who is trying to promote change, and from Jackie's perspective, as the one who appears to be resisting. This activity is designed to create deeper understanding of and more empathy for Jackie, so that participants can generate more creative suggestions about what Paula might do to support Jackie in her teaching.

Large-group discussion (30–40 minutes)

Direct participants' attention to the first scene of the case and, if necessary, ask that they reread this scene. Focus on Jackie's response to Paula's delivery of the tangrams. First, describe the behavior, trying to use nonjudgmental language. Post this description on an overhead or on newsprint for all to see. One version of the behavior in the first scene might be "When Paula brings Jackie tangrams for her class, Jackie responds politely but doesn't talk with Paula about them or their use."

Then ask participants to speculate about the internal conversation or the unspoken thoughts that Jackie, and then Paula, might have had as a result of this action. Encourage participants to use evidence from the text (subsequent conversations with other characters, like Gail or the mathematics specialists, as well as textual references to what Jackie or Paula were thinking). They should also try to move beyond the case text to suggest other ideas these two characters might have had or feelings they might have experienced at this point. Suggest that participants speak in the first person as Jackie or Paula ("I'm concerned about . . ." or "I feel . . ."). Ask the following question:

■ If we could eavesdrop in this particular encounter on what Jackie or Paula was thinking but not saying, what might we hear?

Participants might offer many versions of Jackie's internal conversation while she responds politely but doesn't talk with Paula about the tangrams. These ideas won't, and shouldn't, be completely consistent with one another. In fact, you should encourage participants to suggest alternatives that are angrier or more thoughtful or more revealing than the ones already on the list. In this way, you help expand

The following thoughts might be part of Jackie's internal conversation:

- *I don't have time to do anything else new this year, because working with this new curriculum is hard enough.*

- *I need to go at my own pace, and I feel that Paula is pushing me.*

- *I'm having a harder time than I thought figuring out how third grade works, and I'm a little embarrassed about that.*

- *I don't like having other people poke their nose into what's happening in my classroom.*

- *I am interested in tangrams and thought Paula's demonstration was interesting, but I hadn't really thought about using them myself.*

- *I'm upset that Gail repeated what I said to Paula. What else has Gail been telling other people about me?*

Paula's internal conversation might consist of statements like:

- *That felt like a big brush-off, as if Jackie has no intention of ever using tangrams or any other manipulative. I guess she's just too set in her ways to try anything new.*

- *Jackie seems really touchy over any suggestions about her teaching. I can't even imagine how she'd react if I offered to do a demonstration lesson with her class.*

- *Did she get up on the wrong side of the bed this morning, or what?!*

- *I'm just trying to figure out how I can open up a conversation with Jackie about what she's doing in her classroom. If tangrams don't do it, maybe something else will.*

- *This probably wasn't the best time to drop the tangrams off, since she's distracted getting ready for the start of the day.*

The ideas the group generates about Jackie's and Paula's internal conversations might be recorded in two columns (Jackie and Paula) or, recorded in the order in which they were offered and labeled J or P. Or the ideas might be discussed but not recorded until everyone has had a chance to suggest one. How you as the facilitator manage the discussion should be informed by the line of inquiry you want the group to follow. If you want participants to become aware of Jackie's and Paula's very different interpretations of the same behavior and to develop some sensitivity to this fact, then asking for ideas but not recording them or recording them only in a cursory fashion would probably suffice. If you want participants to work with these differing interpretations, then you will need to organize the ideas in some way (two columns, highlighting key ideas for Jackie or Paula) so that participants can refer them more easily in follow-up activities.

the range of possible interpretations of Jackie's reaction and present more alternatives for Paula to consider in responding to Jackie.

After considering Jackie's and Paula's internal conversations, ask participants to respond to the following questions:

- What might Jackie be resisting?
- What are the ramifications of Paula's assumptions about what Jackie's response means?
- How might Paula find out what Jackie's resistance to the tangrams is about?

Pair discussion (20–40 minutes)

Ask participants to form pairs and take on the character of either Paula or Jackie. This is an opportunity to try out different alternatives to the story line of the case as it is written, using some of the suggestions raised in the preceding large-group discussion. Suggest that the pairs replay the case at three different points:

1. At the beginning of the case. What else might Paula say to Jackie at the outset?
2. After Jackie takes the tangrams and comments that her use of them "depends on whether I can find the place and time in my lessons." What else might Paula say in order to understand what Jackie's comment means?
3. During the week following the Saturday morning mathematics specialist meeting, when Paula seeks Jackie out to talk with her. What could Paula say to open the conversation with Jackie?

In the same pairs, ask participants to speak as their character at these different points. This is the chance to explore and understand resistance from Jackie's and then Paula's point of view.

In the same pairs, ask participants to consider the kind of advice or support that Bob or Faith might offer Paula. Also, consider how Gail might be an ally in dealing with Jackie's resistance. Pose the following questions:

- What advice or help might Bob offer Paula as she works with Jackie?
- What advice or help might Faith offer Paula as she works with Jackie?
- What advice or help might Gail offer Paula as she works with Jackie?

Wrapping Up

This closing activity is designed to help participants arrive at some closure in their work with the case. Adapt the activity described below to fit the case experience you have constructed with participants. How you wrap up the case discussion and what you emphasize will depend on the purpose that you have identified for this case ex-perience. By asking participants to suggest some next steps that the characters might take if the case were extended, you give them the opportunity to integrate their thinking about expert knowledge and expert status into their ideas about working with resistant teachers. Because characters have different perspectives on these issues, encour-age participants to compare and contrast the next steps from the vari-ous characters' points of view.

Small-group discussion (10–15 minutes)

Pose the four questions below on the overhead or on newsprint and ask participants to go to one of the corners of the room, each labeled with one of the questions. Then ask them to consider responses to their specific question, drawing upon what they have discussed in earlier activities. Remind the groups of Bob's interest in having the specialists work with the second-grade teachers in preparation for the state-mandated test at grade two. One strategy the small groups might use during this discussion is to go around the group eliciting one idea from each person. These ideas should be written on an overhead transparency or on newsprint. Ask that the members of each group appoint a spokesperson to present the small group's list to the larger group.

1. At the end of the case, Paula "opened her mouth to respond, and then shut it quickly" after hearing Bob's idea about working with second-grade teachers on the state-mandated test. What could Paula say to Bob and the other mathematics specialists that would express her concerns about expertise and resistance?
2. If Bob and the mathematics specialists agree that it is important to work with the second-grade teachers around the state-mandated test, what are some things they might do?
3. How might the specialist role change if they take on this work with the second-grade teachers? How might their role stay the same? Why?
4. Are there parameters for the specialist role? How are they deter-mined? By whom?

Large-group discussion (20–30 minutes)

Ask spokespersons from each of the small groups to share their re-sponses, beginning with the first question and moving through the other three. In the large-group discussion, encourage participants to compare and contrast the next steps from the various characters' points of view.

CHAPTER 6

From Where I Stand

Case*

Ted Bishop, Principal, Hamilton Elementary School
Beth Daniels, Math mentor and second-grade teacher

Beth Daniels knocked lightly on the frosted glass window of Ted Bishop's open office door. The early morning light from the office windows backlit the word "Principal" written in large script on the glass. The heavy door and old-fashioned glass were relics of an earlier time. "Ted," she asked, "do you have a minute?"

"Come on in, Beth," Ted answered, as he looked up from the piles of papers he was thumbing through on his desk. Beth Daniels, a second-grade teacher and one of three math mentors at Hamilton Elementary School, walked in. Ted continued, "I've been reading through the professional development plans that you and the other teachers turned in a few weeks ago."

"Well, that's connected to what I wanted to talk to you about," replied Beth. "In my professional development plan, I said that I was planning to attend the NCTM conference in April, you know, the National Council of Teachers of Mathematics meeting, that big annual conference that I've gone to the last few years."

"Right," Ted said. "It seems as if that's been a good conference for you."

"It really has," Beth agreed. "Anyway, even though it's a ways off—I mean, the conference is in April and it's only November now—I wanted you to know that I've been thinking about how to cover the costs. I know our professional development budget is small, so I was thinking that I could use my own frequent flyer miles for my plane ticket. But I would want to get reimbursed for the registration fee and

---

*Judith McVarish contributed to the development of this case.

the hotel and things, like before. I thought I could leave on a Wednesday afternoon, after school is out, and return home on Saturday night. That way you'll only need to get a substitute for my class for two days. But, hey, don't worry about remembering all this. I'll write it down for you."

Ted blinked and looked directly at Beth. "Slow down, Beth," he said. "I don't think you requested professional development time to attend that meeting or asked for money to cover your costs. Those forms were all due at the end of October, along with the professional development plans. With all the other requests, I'm not sure there's money for the substitutes and expenses you're talking about."

Taken aback, Beth looked at Ted for a moment. "Ted," she said, "I assumed you would want me to continue attending this conference as part of my role as a math mentor for the building. I mean, I thought that supporting the mentor teachers' attendance at the conference was part of the district's commitment to improving elementary mathematics through teacher leadership."

Ted opened his mouth to reply, but Beth spoke again. "And I don't even think that Katie and Charlie, the other math mentors in the building, are requesting to go to NCTM. But how can you expect us to continue to have leadership positions without even *allowing* us to go to these important conferences?"

"Beth," Ted began as he walked around his desk toward her, "I think your attendance is important, and I know that you need to have professional development experiences in order to continue all your good work as a math mentor. The monthly workshops you've been offering on the early release days have been great, and I love going into classes and seeing teachers use some of the math materials that you've introduced to them. But you know that our professional development funds took a big hit in this year's budget. I'd need three times as much money as I have to meet all the professional development requests that were submitted in October."

Beth shook her head impatiently. "Ted, I know that we're working with less money this year for professional development. We all know that. But this is about the math mentor work. I think that deserves some kind of consideration, don't you? I mean, I'm doing a lot of work here in the building. I guess I must have regular contact with almost a third of the teachers here, besides running the Family Math program. I'd think that the least you could do is support me by helping me get to a conference like NCTM!"

"Beth, this isn't about whether you do good work or not," Ted replied. "You know I think you're doing a great job as a math mentor. But I have to allocate professional development funds for all the teachers in the building. Right now, it's looking as if April will be a really busy month. I've already committed three days of release time for each of the five kindergarten teachers to attend the primary whole language conference at the beginning of April, and the fourth-grade teachers are going again this year to an environmental education institute a week later. With those requests, we're at the substitute limit for the month, and I've already had to juggle some things to find the money to cover the costs for those two conferences."

Beth looked at Ted for a moment. "Ted, I don't know what to say. I think it's important to go to the NCTM Annual Meeting, and that makes it sound as if I think the kindergarten teachers shouldn't go to the whole language conference and that environmental education isn't important!"

"I'm don't want you to argue that your conference is more important than other professional development, Beth," Ted said slowly. "It's my job to try to stretch our professional development funds as far as I can and to try to support as many people as I can in this building."

He paused, and then continued. "I think your work as a math mentor is very important, and I'll do what I can to help you out. Look, it's only November. Let's wait until closer to April to make a final decision. I'll have a better sense of how the professional development spending is looking. I might be able to finagle the subs for those two days, but you'd probably have to cover the registration and housing costs. I'm sorry, Beth, but that's the best I can do right now."

Silent, Beth turned to leave, and then reconsidered. "Ted," she said firmly, "we both know change takes a long time. This district has to find ways to support teachers on a long-term basis. And, quite frankly, I need to know that I can count on support from my building principal. You're right, I should have submitted the professional development request on time, but I assumed it was part of my mentor role to go, and there is no point in going into all the possible excuses now. I'll admit to my error, but it makes me wonder whether this district values math mentors and the role we play to make math reform happen around here." Beth turned sharply on her heel and walked out the door.

■ ■ ■

Late that afternoon, Ted stood up from his desk and stretched wearily. He looked at his watch. It was 4:30, and he still had a 6:30 school council meeting with parent, community, and teacher representatives. His day had started with a parents' coffee at 7:30 in the morning.

He hadn't really been prepared to jump into a debate about cooperative learning at that hour of the morning, with Mrs. Krenshaw of all people. Some of the parents were uncomfortable with ideas that seemed unfamiliar to them, just as some of the teachers were. He re-called the sixth-grade teachers he had met with at lunch, who were unhappy with the pullout strategy implemented this year to buy some time for the instrumental music program. They didn't like the many interruptions it caused in the day and the fact that they couldn't count on seeing the same kids for three periods a week. Ted agreed with them. It was tough to teach the academic program when students were moving in and out of class, but parents had really advocated for an instrumental music program during the day, and the bus schedules made it practically impossible to run the program after school.

Ted walked over to the table under the windows and picked up a few samples of fifth graders' autobiographies. A pile of number lines the first graders had made threatened to spill onto the floor. He tried to remember when these pieces of student work had appeared in his office. He spent far too much of his time dealing with things that kept him out of the classrooms and away from what students were doing. This morning's meeting with the superintendent was a good example.

Ted had gone to talk with the superintendent, Jim Kelly, about options for budgeting that would give more authority and funds to the individual schools, so that principals could have more discretion in allocating money for professional development and materials. Instead, the superintendent began with questions about the low math scores on the standardized testing from late spring. Computation scores were lower across the whole district, but Hamilton's scores were the lowest.

Jim Kelly was usually a hands-off kind of administrator when it came to instructional programs, but Ted thought he was asking some pretty challenging questions about whether Hamilton's math program was very effective. Ted pointed out that scores on concept develop-ment and problem solving had remained the same or improved slightly from the previous year, but he suspected that Kelly was echo-ing the concerns he heard from the middle schools that students wouldn't know enough of the basic skills to do well there.

His conversation with Beth earlier that morning had only added to his worries for the day. Ted shook his head as he recalled Beth's tone of voice in their conversation about her attendance at the NCTM meeting. He knew she would be angry about this for a while. Ted valued the work Beth did as a math mentor and had told her on many occasions that her support of the teachers at Hamilton was important. Yet he suspected that his praise for her work was falling on deaf ears.

Ted wished Beth could see that at the moment his hands were tied. He couldn't manufacture money to cover the costs of everything that teachers wanted to do, and he wasn't very optimistic that Jim Kelly would be allocating more money to professional development during a budget-cutting phase. He was frustrated that there weren't funds for Beth's request and worried that Beth would take the situation personally and not see it as a policy issue.

■ ■ ■

Beth walked down the empty hallway at 5:30, still upset from her encounter with Ted Bishop earlier in the day. After a meeting like that, what was she still doing at school until 5:30 at night preparing for tomorrow's early-release-day workshop?

Beth found it hard to believe that Ted wouldn't want her to go to the NCTM conference. It was one of the few chances she had to talk with folks from other districts who were trying to do some new things in mathematics. She struggled to find time to even talk with Charlie and Katie in her own building and was rarely able to talk with the other math mentors in the district about what was happening in the different schools. It seemed strange to have to leave town in order to be able to talk with people in the same district, not to mention the colleagues she had met across the country.

Beth knew that Ted meant well and had been supportive of her math mentor work in the past. At first it had bothered her when he would pop into her classroom and ask questions about what she was doing, but Beth knew that he was figuring out what they were trying to change in teaching mathematics. She had heard Ted encouraging other teachers to try some of the new strategies that she and the other mentors were promoting or to use some of the manipulatives they were distributing to the classrooms. Beth had thought of Ted as a kind of roving ambassador for math in the building.

Given Ted's obvious interest in math and in her work as a mentor, why was it so difficult for her to get the kind of support she needed now? Beth knew that missing the deadline for the professional development request forms was her fault, but she found it hard to believe that Ted wouldn't assume that she would want to go to NCTM again this year. She needed the opportunity to spend some time learning from her colleagues, to get some professional development for herself of the kind she was always offering to others. Ted was the principal. He understood better than she did what kinds of funds were available for professional development and the many requests made by other teachers. She didn't want to compete with other teachers, but she did want support for her work as a math mentor. If teachers were trying to change the way they taught mathematics, what were principals trying to change? What were *their* responsibilities?

Facilitator's Guide

Summary of the Case

Beth Daniels, a math mentor and second-grade teacher, and Ted Bishop, her building principal, are in the midst of a disagreement. Beth wants to attend the annual meeting of the National Council of Teachers of Mathematics because she sees the opportunity for networking and sharing among colleagues as critical to her role as the math mentor for her building. Unfortunately, Beth has missed the deadline for professional development funding requests and Ted isn't sure that he'll be able to support Beth's attendance.

Beth leaves the meeting upset about what she sees as Ted's limited support for her math mentor work, which she does in addition to her full-time teaching responsibilities. Her conversation with Ted leads her to wonder about the extent of the school's commitment to math mentors.

At the same time, Ted continues to consider Beth's request relative to the many other demands upon his time that day. His ideas about the level of resources and support for math mentors and other worthy programs, raise new questions about the relationship between building principal and math mentor and underscore the isolation that each is experiencing.

Leadership Themes

In this case, we see the dynamics between a principal and a teacher leader, each committed to reform and each seeking support for his or her respective efforts. Although there are many opportunities for finding common ground, we get the sense that Beth's view and Ted's view of the situation are quite different.

In particular, the case offers the opportunity to explore questions about

- *Building support among administrators:* What kinds of support do teacher leaders need from administrators? What kinds of support can teacher leaders offer to administrators?
- *Securing resources and policy support:* What kind of resources do teacher leaders require to sustain themselves and their efforts? How are these resources similar to and different from the resources teachers need to change their classroom practice?

Summary of Activities

This guide offers six sets of suggested activities designed to support discussion of the case. You should feel free to add or delete activities, adapt them to suit your purposes, or resequence them to fit the needs of the participants. As presented here, the sets of activities are structured to focus first on the content of the case itself and then to consider larger issues beyond the immediate case scenario related to the leadership themes. Estimates of the total amount of time needed, if one were to do all the activities in a set, are indicated in parentheses. Time estimates for individual activities are found in the descriptions that follow.

The six sets of activities are as follows:

- *Getting Started:* A large-group discussion of alternative case titles to consider the range and variety of issues contained in the case (20–30 minutes)
- *Understanding Perspectives:* Small- and large-group discussions to explore the perspectives of Beth and Ted on leadership roles (45–60 minutes)
- *Securing Resources and Policy Support:* Small-group discussion followed by two rounds of large-group discussion about resources and policies that could support Beth in her math mentor work, ending with small-group discussion about resources and policies in participants' own contexts (50–70 minutes)
- *Building Support:* An individual activity followed by triad and large-group discussion about the various people who might provide a support network for teacher leadership work (40–55 minutes)
- *Shaping School Culture:* Silent reading of an article that applies ideas about school culture to the case and to participants' own schools, followed by small-group discussion (30–40 minutes)
- *Wrapping Up:* Individual reflection and large-group discussion on the support that teacher leaders and administrators offer to one other (15–25 minutes)

Getting Started

These questions are designed to help participants focus on the kinds of issues the case raises. The purpose is not to come to a definitive answer ("it's about *this* issue"), but to illustrate the fact that participants find a range of issues worth discussing in this one case. Because of this, it will be important as a facilitator for you to try to link issues together, looking for logical connections or identifying issues that seem to break new ground.

Large-group discussion (20–30 minutes)

Distribute an index card to each participant and ask that each person write a new title for the case using as few words as possible. Suggest beginning with "The Case of . . ." in the spirit of the late 1950s television show, *Perry Mason.*

After participants have had time to write a title on the index card, ask them to pass the index cards around their table (or other natural grouping). Collect the pack of index cards from one table and pass it along to another table, continuing in this way until all participants have read each other's index cards. Ask each participant to jot brief notes as they read the index cards so they remember the titles they think are

Some facilitators have been known to hum the dramatic theme song to the old Perry Mason *TV show to reinforce this idea. The point of this activity is for participants to be economical in their titles. Completing the phrase "The Case of . . ." means creating a title that would fit on a book cover or fill the space of a television screen and no more.*

most appropriate as well as any titles about which they have questions or would like discussion. After the index cards have been passed around, begin the large-group discussion with questions such as

- Which title did you think best captured the essence of this case? Why?
- Did any of these titles share one particular focus?
- What questions did you have about a particular title, especially if you thought it was intriguing but weren't quite sure of its meaning?

In the course of discussing titles, try to listen for any confusion about the story line and the details of the case. Listen for those that are popular or ask for a show of hands ("How many of you made a note of this title?"). Ask participants to clarify points in the case, using evidence to illustrate their thinking. Keep participants focused on the facts of the case (Beth is a full-time classroom teacher and a math mentor) rather than on their opinions about the case (Ted should realize that Beth has too many things on her mind, so it's understandable that she might forget the October deadline).

Understanding Perspectives

In this case we hear from two characters: Beth Daniels, a math mentor and classroom teacher, and Ted Bishop, an elementary school principal. Traditionally, there is little overlap between the responsibilities of a teacher and those of a principal. However, as a math mentor, Beth also has leadership responsibilities, and thus does have something important in common with Ted. The activities in this section provide opportunities to explore Ted's and Beth's perspectives on their leadership roles and to consider the ways in which their leadership responsibilities and interests are similar and different.

Small-group discussion (15–20 minutes)

Divide the larger group into small discussion groups of four to five people. This activity has two components. The first is to understand each character's view of his or her own leadership responsibilities and interests (e.g., what does Beth think about herself as a leader—Beth on Beth; what does Ted think about himself as a leader—Ted on Ted). The second is to understand each character's expectations of the other as a leader (e.g., what does Beth think about Ted as a leader—Beth on Ted; what does Ted think about Beth as a leader—Ted on Beth).

Encourage participants to use evidence from the case to back up their assertions about Beth's and Ted's views on leadership. Ask groups to address the following questions:

1. Beth on Beth: What are Beth's responsibilities as a math mentor? What does she want in order to be more effective?
2. Beth on Ted: What expectations does Beth have of Ted as a leader in the school and the district?

If the group comprises fewer than fifteen people, you might try a variation of the index card activity in which participants print their titles on 3 × 5 Post-it notes using markers to make them easy to read. Post these on a piece of newsprint in a designated area for everyone to read and consider. While people are gathered to read the Post-its, you can begin discussing categories, physically moving the Post-its to reflect these categories.

A natural temptation for participants at this early point in the discussion is to want to offer solutions to the compelling dilemma at the end of the case. The challenge for you as the facilitator is to keep participants on track defining the problem in the case—it is more important to identify the range of issues in the case than to move into solving one particular problem.

The current reform movement presents principals with both challenges and opportunities. A growing literature describes how leadership is negotiated, and often shared, by principals, teacher leaders, and teachers. This often involves developing new role expectations and new power relationships. See, for example, Fullan (1993, 1997), Sebring and Bryk (1998), and Smylie and Brownlee-Conyers (1992).

3. Ted on Ted: What are Ted's responsibilities as a principal? What does he want in order to be more effective?

4. Ted on Beth: What expectations does Ted have of Beth as a leader in the school?

Large-group discussion (30–40 minutes)

In the large-group setting, draw on the work of the small groups to discuss what Beth and Ted think about leadership. Pose the four questions above and ask participants to volunteer their ideas and record them in the appropriate sections of a table (see Figure 6.1). (Create a large table by taping sheets of newsprint together to record the responses of all the small groups or a smaller table on a single piece of newsprint or overhead transparency for a synthesis of ideas from many groups.)

The examples in Figure 6.1 are only illustrative. Participants may contribute other ideas or you, as the facilitator, may want to highlight other observations.

As the participants fill in the table, discuss the similarities between the two perspectives (e.g., both Beth and Ted believe that their efforts contribute to improved math programs; both are seeking more financial support for their efforts) and the differences (e.g., Beth identifies her leadership role as primarily in the school while Ted is exploring his leadership role in the district as well as in the school).

Figure 6.1: Perspectives on Leadership Roles

	Beth	*Ted*
Beth on	1.	2.
	–introduces new math materials to colleagues –runs Family Math night –works with 2 other math mentors in the building –wants opportunities to network with other teacher leaders (e.g., at NCTM annual meeting)	–expects Ted to access and use professional development resources to support teachers, especially math mentors –wants Ted to acknowledge her leadership responsibilities by securing resources to help her in her mentor work
Ted on	4.	3.
	–expects Beth to work with colleagues to change classroom practice –wants Beth to realize that some of the same constraints that make change in classrooms tough also make changes in district policy tough	–oversees professional development plans for teachers –actively encourages teachers to try new math instructional practices –wants more school-based control over budgets and more funds

Consider the following questions:

- How would Ted and Beth complete the following statements?
  As a leader, a principal is someone who _____.
  As a leader, a math mentor is someone who _____.
- What statements would Ted and Beth agree on? What would they view differently?
- What beliefs about leadership do Ted and Beth share?

You might extend the discussion by asking participants to focus on a third leadership position, that of superintendent, since it can be easier to explore common ground and shared beliefs about leadership when looking at a third party. In addition to the limited information in the case about Jim Kelly, the district superintendent, participants will need to draw on their own expectations and experiences to respond to the following questions:

You might ask participants to add another column and row to the table for Jim. You might choose to focus on how Ted sees Jim as a leader and how Jim sees Ted as a leader. Filling in the additional sections on the table could serve as preparation for discussing the questions.

- How would Ted and Beth complete the following statement?
  As a leader, a superintendent is someone who _____.
- What might Jim want in order to be more effective?

Securing Resources and Policy Support

Whether they are teacher leaders or principals, in order to be successful leaders need access to the resources that help them do the best possible job. These resources are generally available (or not) because of school or district policies. Understanding what resources and policies might promote teacher leadership and learning how to influence the availability of resources through policy development is important to the success of teacher leadership.

Small-group discussion (10–15 minutes)

Ask participants to form small groups with people they haven't worked with before. The purpose of this small-group discussion is to brainstorm ideas about leadership resources that can be shared in the large group. The following questions are designed to help participants identify and discuss the resources and policies that affect teacher leadership. Encourage participants to think broadly and creatively about resources, considering materials, finances, time, and personnel. Use evidence from the case to respond to the questions.

- What resources are available to Beth in her work as a math mentor?
- What additional resources might Ted have access to that could help Beth be more effective in her work? Why would these resources be useful?
- What additional resources could Beth and Ted work together to obtain? Why would these be useful resources?

While you might choose to discuss any one of these resources in more depth, you might also ask to hear the range of possible resources, to emphasize their variety and quantity, before moving to questions about policies.

You may want to suggest some kinds of policies to get discussion started—policies about time (release time for teacher leaders and teachers, time allocated for professional development and planning), meetings (faculty meetings, grade-level meetings), funds (for professional development costs, materials, substitutes), or community outreach (creating business partnerships, accessing community resources, securing funds outside the district).

Large-group discussion (25–35 minutes)

Bring participants together in the larger group and ask each small group to identify one resource they believe Beth has available or might have available in her work as a math mentor. Make a list on newsprint or an overhead transparency for this discussion and for the upcoming discussion of policy. Continue to solicit one idea from each small group until there are no new ideas to contribute.

Pose the following questions:

- What is one resource that is available to Beth or could be available to Beth in her work as a math mentor?
- How do you know? What evidence do you find in the case?
- What resources could Ted provide?
- What resources could Ted and Beth secure together?

Since the availability of resources is often dependent on school or district policies, ask participants in the large-group setting to consider the policies in schools and across the district that support teacher leadership or make it difficult. Again, encourage participants to think broadly and creatively about policies.

Use the list of resources compiled earlier to consider the following questions:

- What policies support Beth in her work as a math mentor?
- What policies could Ted change or influence that could provide additional support to Beth in her work as a math mentor? How would these new policies support her work?
- What policies could Beth and Ted work together to shape? How would these policies support her work as a math mentor?

An often overlooked resource is the time within the school day. Frequently, regularly scheduled faculty meetings, department meetings, or grade-level meetings do not use time very well, and participants could consider this issue as a possible resource for supporting the work of teacher leaders. In many schools, time can be "found" by reconfiguring the school schedule to carve out common planning times or to ensure that teacher leaders are available to work with particular teachers. If these resources, and the policies through which to access these resources, have not come up in the conversation, suggest them.

Small-group discussion (15–20 minutes)

Continue the discussion by moving beyond the case and the characters of Beth and Ted to the participants' own situations. Ask participants to respond to these questions in small groups:

- Think about your school or district. What resources that support teacher leadership are most plentiful? How do or how could teacher leaders use these resources?

- What additional resources would be helpful to teacher leaders in their work? What policies affect the availability of these resources? Who can influence these policies?

Building Support

Teacher leaders can be more effective in their work, and experience greater satisfaction, when they work with others (and receive support for their efforts) rather than work in isolation. We usually think about getting support from individuals who understand our efforts and agree with our ideas. These individuals are valuable because they can be real advocates for our work. However, they are not the only ones who can provide support. This activity asks participants to consider a variety of individuals who can support teacher leadership efforts.

Individual written reflection (15–20 minutes)

In this activity participants are asked to think about two different dimensions of support: agreement and trust. Both are helpful in building support, and yet support networks can also consist of individuals with different levels of agreement and/or trust. Networks are larger and stronger when they include different points of view.

Consider what it would mean to build a support network for *your* work. By *agreement*, we mean approval of your efforts, promotion of your activities, or concurrence with your actions. There are people who agree with you and your work (high agreement) and individuals who disagree with you and your work (low agreement). You can get support from both groups, although the support will look different. By *trust*, we mean the assurance of someone's backing, an expression of faith in your ideas or confidence in your approach. There are people whom you trust and who trust you (high trust) as well as those whom you distrust (low trust). Both groups of people are capable of providing support but, again, the support will look different.

In this activity, ask participants to think about the various individuals from whom they can receive or cultivate support for teacher leadership work and to record the names of these individuals in the appropriate section of a table (see Figure 6.2).

Triads discussion (15–20 minutes)

After participants have worked individually on their agree/trust table to identify supporters of teacher leadership work, ask them to form groups of three to compare notes and to discuss how these kinds of support can help the work of teacher leaders.

Pose the following questions:

- How widespread is your support network? Was it easy to think of individuals for each of the four sections of the table?
- Is there a pattern to the kinds of individuals who appear on the table? Why?

The activity is set up as though participants are themselves teacher leaders or are working with teacher leaders, but it can also focus on Beth, the teacher leader in the case, and conjecture about the kinds of people who might support her in her math mentor work.

These ideas are adapted from Block (1987) and McGonagill (1995).

	High trust	Low trust
High agreement		
Low agreement		

You might want to prepare a mock-up of the table, summarizing what the different levels of agreement and trust mean in each section, as described in Figure 6.2. This table could be drawn on newsprint, or on an overhead transparency, or passed out as an individual handout.

Figure 6.2: Support Network

A support network can consist of people other than those with whom we have complete agreement and deep trust. Since teacher leaders typically interact with many others who fall short of this ideal, it is useful to consider what kinds of support these others can offer. The descriptors for the four table sections ask participants to think more broadly about the kind of support various people can offer to teacher leaders.

High agreement/high trust: Some individuals are the stereotypical supporters. They agree with our work and our efforts, and there is mutual trust between us. These people can offer sympathetic advice, they can join us in carrying out our work in the same spirit, and they need minimal explanation of our intentions because they share our point of view.

Low agreement/high trust: Some people can be sounding-board supporters. We trust them, but they don't agree with our actions. We can ask these people to share their perspective to help us understand why they (and others) don't agree with our work. Because we trust them, we can be candid with them and gain insights that will help us in our work with others.

High agreement/low trust: Some individuals can be political supporters. They agree with us, but for a variety of reasons we don't necessarily trust them. We need to be clear about what we want from these people in terms of working together and also about what they want from us. Agreeing on how we can work together productively, with no expectations that they will go beyond these boundaries, is key.

Low agreement/low trust: Some people can be negative supporters or offer no support at all. They don't agree with us and there is little to no mutual trust. This should refer to only a very small number of people, and we shouldn't categorize individuals in this way without some genuine effort to explore the disagreement and investigate whether it is possible to build a more trusting relationship. However, if you conclude that there is low agreement and low trust, then you need to let go of these people as potential supporters; be clear about the ways in which you might have contributed to the current low agreement and low trust, and try to be aboveboard with them about your plans so that you don't undermine their efforts.

- How can you make use of the support these individuals could offer? Cite specific ideas about the support you might get for your teacher leadership work.

Large-group discussion (10–15 minutes)

Bring the triads together in the larger group and ask participants to report on responses to the last question. In this way, everyone will have a chance to hear about specific ways in which different individuals, with varying levels of agreement and trust, can support the work of teacher leaders.

Shaping School Culture

Reform flourishes in schools where the culture supports change efforts. Critical to this culture is active and engaged leadership. This activity asks participants to think about Hamilton Elementary, the school portrayed in the case, as well as their own schools as cultures that promote or impede continuous improvement.

Individual reading (10–15 minutes)

Ask participants to read "What Leaders Need to Know About School Culture" (Norris 1994, reproduced in Appendix B), paying particular attention to the seven mechanisms for shaping school culture discussed at the end of the article.

Small-group discussion (20–25 minutes)

Ask participants to form small groups to discuss the Norris article, focusing on "stuck" and "forward-moving" schools. Think about how these ideas apply to the culture of Hamilton Elementary, the school featured in the case. Since the case does not offer a lot of information about the school, participants will need to make some inferences, which may say as much about their own experiences of school culture as it does about Hamilton.

Ask participants to respond to the following questions:

- In what ways is Hamilton a "forward-moving" school? In what ways is it a "stuck" school?
- Which mechanisms for shaping school culture seem to be currently in use at Hamilton Elementary? Which mechanisms for shaping school culture could be used at Hamilton Elementary? How?
- What should the leaders at Hamilton Elementary—principal and teacher leaders—focus on to shape a positive, forward-thinking school?

Wrapping Up

This closing activity is designed to help participants arrive at some closure to their work with the case. Adapt the activity to fit the case experience you have constructed with participants. How you wrap up the case discussion and what you emphasize will depend on the purpose you have identified for this case experience.

Individual reflection (5–10 minutes)

Pass out large Post-it notes in two colors to each participant and ask everyone to write one important kind of support that teacher leaders need from administrators on one color Post-it and one important kind of support that teacher leaders offer to administrators on the other color Post-it. Around the room, hang large sheets of newsprint labeled "Teacher Leader support offered to Administrators" and "Administrator support for Teacher Leaders." Ask participants to attach their Post-it responses on the appropriate sheet of newsprint.

This activity could be used as a homework assignment to move from this case to another one to be discussed at a later date.

The same questions can be used to focus on participants' own school settings.

Large-group discussion (10–15 minutes)

Ask participants to look at the responses under each of the two headings. Discuss the relative number of responses and the different kinds of support that one group can offer the other. Focus the discussion to consider reciprocity of support—from teacher leaders to administrators and from administrators to teacher leaders—as an important outcome. Use the following questions for discussion:

■ Which heading has the larger number of responses? Why?

■ What would it take for us, as a group, to increase the number of responses under either of these categories?

■ Are the kinds of support that teacher leaders can offer administrators different in important ways from the support that administrators can offer teacher leaders? Why?

■ Are they similar in important ways? Why?

■ Is it important that there be reciprocal support between teacher leaders and administrators?

CHAPTER 7

Where Do We Go Next?

Case

Emily Gardner, Director of staff development, Fairfield Public Schools
Abigail McCarthy, Director of curriculum
Peter Albright, Business representative
Jake Zelman, Parent volunteer
Peggy Solinski, Math resource teacher
Denise Wyatt, Fourth-grade teacher
Susan Hamilton, Parent volunteer
Jim Michelson, Building principal
Talbot Kent, School board representative

Emily Gardner, director of staff development for the Fairfield Public Schools, walked down the long, empty corridor toward the media center thinking about the district math advisory committee meeting. "It's been great having a cadre of math resource teachers in the elementary schools, and doing it with the support of this advisory group has made a difference. One of the most significant things we've done is to demonstrate that community involvement does work. Getting input from folks who aren't in the classroom has been really valuable, especially since we had to jump into this work quickly once we got district money to develop this group of teacher leaders three years ago. That original design—of finding a person in each of our nineteen elementary schools who would become a resource teacher—made a lot of sense."

Emily turned the corner and headed toward the open doors of the media center. "Unfortunately," she thought, frowning slightly, "what seemed like a simple idea—providing support to teachers—has turned into something more complicated. Perhaps we're a victim of our own success and we've gone as far as we can go right now. Abigail wants to move ahead with another proposal for funding to train more resource teachers, but is that really what we need to do right now?"

Emily entered the media center and slipped into a chair opposite Abigail McCarthy, the district's curriculum director and Emily's partner in this project. She and Abigail smiled at each other, and both looked around the room at the six other committee members gathered at the table.

Abigail cleared her throat. "It's four o'clock, so why don't we start our meeting? Talbot Kent isn't here yet, but he left a message that he would be a bit late, since he's coming from a school board task force meeting. It's good to see everyone else. I know we haven't had a formal advisory meeting yet this year, and Emily and I are sorry about the lapse." Abigail glanced over at Emily, who nodded in agreement. "We believe our efforts to develop a group of mathematics resource teachers have been coming along well. We continue to hear good things from the elementary schools about the work the resource teachers are doing, especially their demonstration lessons and their leadership of the math committee in their buildings. And, of course, their help in ordering and organizing math materials has made a big difference. Even though we feel we're on track with some of our original goals, we've still been talking about next steps. We want to do some brainstorming with you today about the question Where do we want to go next?"

After a brief silence, Peter Albright, the committee's business representative, spoke up. "I agree that we need to think about next steps, but that's a big question. I'd like to know why it has come up for you two just now, and if you have any suggestions about what we should do."

Abigail nodded. "Sure, Peter, I think that's a good place to start. We have the opportunity to write another proposal for funds—well, two proposals, actually. One would go to our state department of education for Eisenhower funds and another, smaller request would be submitted to the district as part of the budget planning process for next year. Both proposals are due in the next month or so, but before we started writing we wanted to talk with you about some issues related to the math resource teachers. First, our current resource teachers are a fabulous group, but to be perfectly honest, we're worried that they're burning themselves out. They have been on the front lines of helping to change the way math is taught in Fairfield's classrooms for quite a while. As you know, this resource role is in addition to their full-time classroom teaching responsibilities. The hope we had that they would be given release time to do their resource work and to participate in ongoing professional development just hasn't happened. They end up holding important planning meetings after their own classes, at the end of a long day of teaching, and attending inservice sessions after school or on weekends.

"The second issue we're facing," Abigail continued, "is that our original model of having one resource person in each building has been altered somewhat. At this point in time, over a quarter of our resource teachers are teaching in different buildings, so that now we have two, or even three, resource teachers in one building and none in others."

Jake Zelman, the parent of a third-grade student, responded immediately. "Well, this sounds simple enough. I say write the proposals and let's bring more teachers on board!"

"It's not that simple, Jake," Peggy Solinski, a resource teacher, said firmly.

Jake looked at her quizzically. "What do you mean, not that simple? I thought we were in agreement that this program had been a success, that having a designated teacher in each elementary building was working. Why shouldn't we support training more teachers to be resource teachers, especially if our current group needs some relief, like Abigail said, and we have buildings without any resource teachers?"

"Well, take me for example," Denise Wyatt, a fourth-grade teacher responded. "This is my fourth year of teaching, and I'm still feeling as if there isn't enough time to do a good job with all aspects of my teaching. I think math is important and I want things to change, but math isn't the only thing I teach. Look, I couldn't even think about adding the resource teacher work on top of all of that."

Peggy Solinksi nodded. "I think we may have developed unrealistic expectations because of the current group of math resource teachers. We didn't get any release time to do what we were asked to do, and yet somehow we did it. So, everyone expects *all* resource teachers to continue teaching in their own classrooms and at the same time be a resource to other teachers about teaching math in a different way." She leaned forward in her chair and looked intently at the other committee members at the table. "I don't think that preparing more math resource teachers is going to get us anywhere, except to produce more frustration among more math resource teachers. Maybe everyone would be better off—the resource teachers and regular classroom teachers—if everyone was trained in math reform, not just the resource teachers."

Emily quickly spoke up. "I've wondered the same thing, Peggy. I've been asking myself for some time now whether we should bring more teachers into the resource role if we don't have the structures in place to support them."

Abigail countered, "But Emily, we both know that the resource teacher's role *has* made a difference in the buildings. I don't think we have reason to change the model now. We have seen important changes and we don't want the work to stop."

As silence fell in the room, Talbot Kent walked in and sat down next to Peter Albright, murmuring his apologies for being late.

"Abigail?" parent representative Susan Hamilton asked somewhat tentatively. "I have something from a parent's perspective I would like to share."

"Go ahead," Abigail responded.

"My child is in second grade now, where there is a mix of students, some of whom had one of the math resource teachers as a teacher and some who didn't. I volunteer once a week in my daughter's classroom so I've really watched the children. The kids who had the resource teacher as their first-grade classroom teacher last year are more self-assured in math. They can take the information the teacher gives, define the problem, and go about solving it, while some of the other children who had the more traditional methods kind of sit and wait for direction. They need help from the teacher the whole way, and reassurance at the end that they have done it. So I'm really going to be concerned if the math resource program doesn't continue."

Abigail smiled gratefully at Susan. "Thank you, Susan. We've observed similar things, and your comments fit with what we've heard from the resource teachers and some other classroom teachers."

Jim Michelson spoke up. "So it's been good for the kids who have a resource teacher in class, and I'm glad that the teacher you talked about, Susan, is at our school, but I'm concerned about the kids you describe who were in the other teachers' classrooms. I don't think this is just a principal's question, but why don't we see the influence of the resource teacher in the other classrooms?"

Abigail frowned and spoke slowly to emphasize her point. "Well, the hard question we have before us is how to keep the momentum for change in math going. I think we have evidence that this model is, for the most part, working; we just need to get more teachers involved. Once that happens, Jim, then your concerns will most likely be taken care of."

The moment Abigail had finished speaking, school board member Talbot Kent began to speak. "I want to ask a question," he said. "Is this something we really need to be doing in our district right now? Will our efforts to reform math get in the way of the other school subjects? I know the superintendent spoke at our last board meeting about efforts the district will need to make to bring our entire K–8 curriculum in alignment with the state-mandated curriculum frameworks. You know we have limited resources—financial and human."

After a moment or two of silence, Peter Albright spoke. "I have been listening with interest to this conversation, and the issue seems to be how best to continue the changes happening in your classrooms around math that you all connect to the resource teacher role. At the same time, I am hearing that the ones who have been the resource teachers since the beginning are running out of steam, that the additional responsibilities of the resource role are becoming too much, and that some teachers are being left out of the reform efforts. I think that's understandable. Our company would have difficulty asking people to do two jobs at once for such a long time. So, if we train more teachers to be resource teachers in the same way, won't we have the same problem in another two years or so unless the rest of the teachers can become less dependent on the resource teachers? Is the basic problem that we haven't found a good way to get more teachers to change what they're doing in their classrooms?"

Leaning back in his chair, Jim Michelson said, "I'm also apprehensive about whether we can get most of the teachers to be anywhere close to where these resource teachers are in terms of math teaching. Because these resource teachers are the ones who volunteered, they are the ones who are really interested in this area. So then I wonder, if these are the only interested ones, can we even get others to become resource teachers, if we decide to stick with that model? Also, Talbot is right that we do have responsibilities in reading and science and other subjects. I'm not sure, ultimately, how far we can get. It doesn't mean I don't want to try or I'm not supportive of Abigail and Emily and their efforts. But there's the reality of life in elementary schools. It ain't all math! And, as long as this policy about no release time continues, I don't know."

"Jim," Talbot Kent responded, "the school board has gone over release time before, and it just isn't an option. Our resources are simply too limited. We can't afford to hire additional substitutes on a permanent basis so the resource teachers can be doing other things."

Emily glanced at her watch and saw that it was getting close to the end of their scheduled meeting. Pointing to her watch, she signaled Abigail, who said, "Well, Emily is giving me the sign that our time is up. Obviously, we haven't resolved our question about next steps. There seem to be more issues here than I thought there might be. What do you think a possible solution might be? The Eisenhower grant deadline is in three weeks. Should we try to reconvene? Emily, what do you think?"

Before Emily could answer, Jim Michelson offered a suggestion. "Why don't we set a meeting date for next Tuesday afternoon at 4 o'clock, here in the media center, and whoever can make it will come to help resolve the issue. I agree that we need to keep this discussion moving."

The others nodded their assent to Jim's plan. "I plan to be at that meeting," Peter Albright said, "but between now and then I would like Emily and Abigail to talk with as many of the current math resource teachers as possible. I would like to know what they think about the situation. Could you two give us a report on what they think should be our next steps?"

"Yes," Emily promised. "We'll talk with the resource teachers before next Tuesday."

■ ■ ■

Abigail looked at Emily, who was seated directly across the table from her. "Emily, I really appreciate your reworking your schedule so we could have a chance to compare notes on what we've heard from the math resource teachers over the last few days about next steps in the program," Abigail said.

"I'm glad you wanted to meet," Emily replied. "You and I have to come to some agreement before we have another public meeting about all of this." She pushed her chair back from the table a bit. "I don't know how you feel, but I thought we were partly to blame for the confusion at the advisory committee meeting last week. We have to address the fundamental question of whether we should continue to build our math program around the resource teacher model or spread any funding we can obtain to train all the teachers now."

Abigail sighed. "Emily, I know we don't exactly see eye to eye on this one. I think it's important to get funding to build a larger pool of resource teachers, since they've served us well so far."

"I don't have a problem with what the resource teachers have done for our math program, and that is what I said at the advisory committee meeting," Emily protested. "My problem is with the district and with school board members like Talbot Kent. Until we can get something done about releasing the resource teachers for planning time or in some way compensating them for their role, trying to recruit more of them is pointless."

"Emily, if we let the visibility of the resource teacher program go, we will lose any chance of getting the school board to reconsider policies on release time or professional development days." Abigail paused, and then continued. "We have run into the release day thing all along the way. But we shouldn't let an opportunity to obtain more funding for mathematics teaching go. We will need those funds to pay for teachers' time in the summer. Change takes time, and we shouldn't alter our course now, when we see signs that it's working. Clearly, it is going to take more time to change the minds of the board members."

Emily shook her head impatiently. "Why go through all the aggravation of putting together a grant proposal for just a few resource teachers when we know we have policies in the district that will keep them from being effective in helping other teachers?"

Abigail looked down at her notes and then up at Emily. "Look," she suggested, "why don't we try to review what we've heard from the resource teachers." Abigail turned a page in her notebook. "I heard concerns over how long it's taking to get some teachers to try some new things in their math classes, and that those teachers really need a lot of support. And, some resource teachers wonder whether there are many other teachers in the district who are ready or willing to assume this role. The issue of time was frequently mentioned, not having enough of it under the present arrangements."

Emily nodded. "That fits with what I heard, but folks were pointing out that without having any release time to do the resource teacher work, we aren't going to get many more teachers in that role, especially if they're not as motivated about math."

"But, I'm also hearing," Abigail replied, "that their role as a resource teacher is important to them and to the students in Fairfield and that they want to continue."

After a few minutes of silence, Emily sighed. "Well, this is certainly a tough situation. What recommendations are we going to make to the advisory committee? What should we say to them tomorrow?"

Facilitator's Guide

Summary of the Case

Emily Gardner, director of staff development, and Abigail McCarthy, curriculum director for the Fairfield Public Schools, are co-chairs of the district's math advisory committee, which consists of teachers, a principal, parents, and other community members. One of the committee's first activities was to develop, with district funds, a cadre of math resource teachers at the elementary grade level. There is general agreement that the resource teachers have been a valuable asset in the schools, although they continue to do this work in addition to their full-time classroom teaching responsibilities.

The math advisory committee meeting opens with Emily and Abigail laying out the various options for the next steps in the resource teacher program. Emily is hesitant to increase the number of resource teachers until the district can offer them more support, while Abigail believes that proposals should be written to secure funds to train more resource teachers. The response from the committee is mixed, as different people raise points about the important work of the resource teachers, the distribution of the resource teachers across all the schools, the availability of district resources, the likelihood of changing policies about release time for resource teachers, and the options for recruiting a second wave of teacher leaders.

Because of the lack of consensus among the committee members, Abigail and Emily agree to gather more information from the current resource teachers and come back to the group's next meeting with a recommendation about the future of resource teacher program. Their attempts to come to agreement on a recommendation reveal the underlying issues about what it takes to make substantive change within a district, given existing resources and policies.

Leadership Themes

This case highlights the challenges of keeping a change effort active beyond the initial implementation phase. Emily, Abigail, and the members of their advisory committee are struggling with what next steps they might take, given the success of the mathematics resource teachers to date. The case portrays different perspectives on how a program like the resource teachers should be developed and supported.

In particular, the case offers the opportunity to explore questions about

- *Developing a critical mass for change*: What constitutes a critical mass for any particular change effort? Are strategies for sustaining change similar to those for promoting change in the first place?

■ *Securing resources/policy support*: What resources are needed to sustain change efforts? At what point should attention be paid to policies in support of change efforts? What perspectives can teacher leaders offer to policy discussions?

Summary of Activities

This guide offers six sets of suggested activities designed to support discussion of the case. You should feel free to add or delete activities, adapt them to suit your purposes, or resequence them to fit the needs of the participants. As presented here, the sets of activities are structured to focus first on the content of the case itself and then to consider larger issues beyond the immediate case scenario related to the leadership themes. Estimates of the total amount of time needed, if one were to do all of the activities in a set, are given in parentheses. Time estimates for individual activities are found in the descriptions that follow.

The six sets of activities are as follows:

■ *Getting Started:* Pairs, squares, and large-group discussion of the range and variety of issues in the case (20–30 minutes)
■ *Understanding Perspectives:* A triad discussion leading to a role play followed by a large-group discussion to explore the perspectives of Emily and Abigail and to articulate the recommendations each might make regarding resource teachers (45–65 minutes)
■ *Developing a Critical Mass for Change:* Optional individual written reflection precedes small- and large-group discussion to investigate various models by which resource teachers build a critical mass among their colleagues (60–80 minutes)
■ *Securing Resources and Policy Support:* A small- and large-group discussion exploring incentives and obstacles to expanding the corps of teacher leaders (30–40 minutes)
■ *Imagining Outcomes:* Large- and small-group discussions to play out various recommendations that the Emily and Abigail might make to the committee (35–55 minutes)
■ *Wrapping Up:* Individual reflection and large-group discussion on the similarities and differences among teacher leadership issues about starting-up versus sustaining a reform initiative (15–25 minutes)

Getting Started

This activity helps participants orient themselves to the case and its story line and get acquainted with the range of issues this case features. The purpose is both to clarify the details of the case by summarizing it and to generate the list of issues to focus later discussion.

Pairs/squares discussion (10–15 minutes)

Divide the group into pairs. Ask each participant to share with his or her partner a brief summary of what happened in the case. After both partners have finished, the pair then turns to another pair sitting close by to share their descriptions with them. The "square" (consisting of four participants or two pairs) discusses the ways in which their descriptions are similar and different. You might use the following questions:

- What are the key points in this story?
- In what way is your description similar to mine? Different from mine?
- Are the differences in our summaries critical? Do they get at different issues?

Large-group discussion (10–15 minutes)

Ask the "squares" to share their descriptions with others in the larger group. Begin by getting a full description from one square, and then ask subsequent squares to add their own ideas (if different from those already reported). Also, ask participants to note new ideas they hadn't thought of themselves but with which they readily agree; questions sparked by participants' descriptions, which they want to return to over the course of the discussion; and examples of shifts in perspective or ways in which other participants' descriptions have caused them to rethink and modify their own descriptions. Record these ideas on a sheet of newsprint divided into thirds. Label one section with a lightbulb to represent the "bright ideas" generated by the discussion, a second section with a series of question marks to note the questions that participants want to track through the discussion, and a third section with a large triangle or delta to record changes or shifts in perspective on the case in this opening discussion.

Use the following questions to help participants share their descriptions in the larger group:

- Do you have anything else to add to the description the first "square" offered?
- Does anyone want to comment on any of the new bright ideas that they're hearing for the first time? What strikes you as interesting or important about these ideas?
- Are there any questions these descriptions are raising for you? What further discussion would you like to have before you return to these questions?
- Have any of you heard anything that is causing you to rethink your original description? What did you hear? What are you now thinking?

A natural pitfall for participants at this early point in the discussion is to want to offer solutions to the compelling dilemma at the end of the case. The challenge for you as the facilitator is to keep participants on track in describing the case and in identifying the issues they see in the case, rather than offering their ideas about how to address these issues. The focus is on defining problems rather than on problem solving, an important step at this early stage of the discussion.

The newsprint with the record of bright ideas, questions, and changes in thinking is useful for focusing attention during the large-group discussion. You can ask participants to identify which type of comment is being made. After the three sections have been completed in the large group, the pairs can meet again to discuss the kinds of issues recorded. If needed, another round of the large-group discussion can record additional bright ideas, burning questions, or shifts in thinking.

Understanding Perspectives

Our perspectives on an issue emerge from our own experiences, information, and personal goals. Because we all have different experiences and take in information in different ways, it is rare that everyone seated around a meeting table (in real life or in this case) will view the decisions to be made in the same way. Even when people have similar points of view, the language they use to describe their own point of view may suggest more dissimilarity than similarity. An important leadership skill is the ability to understand other perspectives without feeling threatened if they differ from your own. Understanding is the first step to building consensus among differing points of view. These activities provide opportunities for participants to sort out and consider the different perspectives of committee members regarding next steps for the mathematics resource teacher program. The case presents many points of view; we recommend that you focus on Emily and Abigail, the characters about whom we know the most, along with one or two of the minor characters. Participants' choice of the minor character—a parent, a mathematics resource teacher, a classroom teacher, a principal, a school board member, or a business representative—should depend on the interests or questions they bring to this case. The discussion questions that follow focus first on understanding the characters' perspectives on the role of resource teachers and the support they require after the initial implementation phase. Then the questions move away from the story line to ask participants to reflect on their own ideas about teacher leaders in the role of resource teachers.

Triad discussion (10–15 minutes)

Divide the large group into groups of three and ask each triad to analyze three characters: Emily, Abigail, and one minor character of their choice. Encourage participants to use evidence from the case and distribute highlighters or colored pencils to them to use in marking the passages where they find evidence in support of their responses. If possible, use different colors for different characters. Ask participants to respond to the following questions from the perspective of each character:

- Under what conditions should resource teachers work? What support should they receive?
- What role do resource teachers play in the overall district program for mathematics education reform?

Role play (15–20 minutes)

One person takes the role of Emily, the other the role of Abigail. The third person is the commentator. The Emily and Abigail characters discuss their responses to the closing lines of the case: "Well, this is certainly a tough situation. What recommendations are we going to

---

You can set up this activity to focus only on Emily and Abigail and leave the minor character for a later discussion. Assign half of the group to Emily and the other half to Abigail. Use the questions for the triad discussion asking everyone to note evidence in the case that explains either perspective. Set up the role play by asking some participants (an equal number from the Emily and the Abigail groups) to take the role of the commentator. Ask the commentators to sit in various places around the room so that an "Emily" and an "Abigail" can join each to form triads for the role play.

make to the advisory committee? What should we say to them tomorrow?" The commentator listens to the role play and comments on the ideas presented by each person, the new information brought to the discussion, and opportunities for finding common ground between the two characters.

Set up the role play in the following way:

1. Emily and Abigail each take a couple of minutes to collect their thoughts about the recommendations each would like to make to the advisory committee. (What would Emily recommend to the committee? Why? What would Abigail recommend to the committee? Why?)
2. The commentator reads the closing lines of the case aloud as a signal for the role play to begin and then keeps time. (The amount of the time can be negotiated. We suggest five minutes.)
3. Emily and Abigail (speaking in the first person) share their ideas about next steps and offer reasons for their ideas as needed.
4. As needed, the commentator prompts Emily and Abigail to elaborate on their ideas or to suggest an idea discussed earlier, encouraging them to talk for the full five minutes.
5. The commentator offers reflections on the role play: What issues were most hotly contested? What new ideas or information were offered? What opportunities might there be for common ground between Emily and Abigail?

The triad should also consider how the minor character might respond to the Emily/Abigail discussion. Discuss the following questions:

- With whom would that minor character be in agreement? Why?
- What new perspective does this character bring to the Emily/Abigail discussion?

Large-group discussion (20–30 minutes)

Begin the large-group discussion by asking the triads to share the recommendations they think Emily and Abigail might make to the advisory committee. On newsprint or an overhead transparency, record the recommendations in two columns, one labeled *Emily* and the other *Abigail*. Include the reasons for the recommendations. Note any similarities among the recommendations as the discussion proceeds. Pose the following questions:

- What was Emily's recommendation to the advisory committee? Why did she hold this view?
- What was Abigail's recommendation to the advisory committee? Why did she hold this view?
- What are the common features in Emily's and Abigail's recommendations?

As participants prepare to take on the role of Emily or Abigail, be mindful that some may be playing a character they don't particularly like or toward whom they feel little sympathy. Encourage participants to try to understand which issues are most important from that character's point of view. It is their job, in the role play, to present Emily's or Abigail's recommendations in the best possible light. The debriefing after the role play might include discussion of how Emily's or Abigail's perspectives compared to their own.

Remind participants that as they consider the recommendations Emily or Abigail might make to the committee, they should stay focused on why a particular recommendation seems advisable and avoid getting caught up in the details of a particular recommendation. The conversation between Emily and Abigail is most productive when they discuss the rationale behind specific recommendations. Why is Emily advocating one recommendation? Why is Abigail presenting a different recommendation? The Emily/Abigail discussion is an opportunity to gain greater clarity on their perspectives, not to engage in problem solving. At this point, it is premature to move toward problem solving in terms of the next steps with the committee.

- What underlying beliefs about resource teachers and their role do Emily and Abigail share? How are these beliefs evidenced in their recommendations?

Ask participants to discuss the views of various minor characters toward Emily's and Abigail's recommendations. Consider what new ideas these minor characters could contribute to the discussion. Under the appropriate *Emily* or *Abigail* column, note the name of the minor character and the contribution that character might make.

For many participants, assuming the role of a character and doing a role play are powerful ways to focus on the perspective of that character. Ask the group to analyze the role-play process itself. Pose the following questions:

- How did the role play feel? What was it like to be Emily? Abigail? the commentator?
- For Emily and Abigail: What helped you stay in character? How much of the other character's comments do you recall?
- For the commentator: What opportunities did you see for finding common ground between Emily and Abigail? Did they see these opportunities? If not, why not?

Developing a Critical Mass for Change

When we talk about creating change in schools, we are talking about influencing a number of people: teachers, students, parents, administrators. Even when we only focus on teachers, such change will only come about and be sustained when sufficient numbers are committed to changing their classroom practice. Teacher leaders are typically called upon to reach out to their colleagues so that changed practice becomes the norm rather than the exception in a school, within a department, or across a grade level. This is what we mean by "critical mass"—enough individuals who understand and are committed to keeping change efforts alive.

Individual written reflection (10 minutes)

Prior to the small-group discussion, ask participants to write in response to one of the following suggested prompts. There may be others that are more germane to participants' situations. Have participants seek out comfortable places to do their reflection and writing.

- Have you been a member of a group like the math advisory committee where there are very different points of view expressed? Was your role like that of one of the committee members? Who? What did it feel like? What were your concerns?
- Write briefly about an experience you have had that gave you insight into how change occurs among teachers in schools. List some of the key features of that experience.

It may be helpful to make connections between this exercise and what might occur during a meeting while you are trying to reach some level of consensus. It can be easier to understand different viewpoints if you spend time imagining others' perspectives.

- Based on your experience, what kind of critical mass is needed for change in school to be sustained? Why?

Small-group discussion (20–30 minutes)

Create small groups of four to five participants. Display on an overhead or on newsprint the following scenarios for utilizing teacher leaders (in this case, resource teachers) and ask participants to consider specific ways in which resource teachers work to create a critical mass for change among colleagues:

- Resource teacher assigned to each school
- Resource teachers deployed on an "as requested" basis
- Resource teachers assigned to grade levels
- Resource teachers working with targeted populations (e.g., new teachers, probationary teachers, teachers implementing new curriculum)

Pose the following questions:

- Who constitutes the critical mass that resource teachers are trying to develop in each scenario?
- How do resource teachers in each scenario build a critical mass of colleagues engaged in change efforts?
- What advantages does each scenario offer in developing a critical mass for change?

Large-group activity (30–40 minutes)

Bring participants back together in the larger group to share the small-group discussion. Ask various small groups to report on each of the four scenarios according to which resource teachers might create a critical mass for change among their colleagues, focusing particularly on the advantages offered by a particular scenario.

Continue the discussion by asking the participants to consider various models of change within groups and how leaders influence change. The scenarios for utilizing teacher leaders, such as resource teachers, are premised on different models for bringing about change. Discussion of these models can help bring underlying assumptions about how change happens to the surface, particularly change among large numbers of people.

Present the picture of each of the models shown in Figures 7.1 to 7.4: (1) telephone model; (2) pyramid or train-the-trainer model; (3) overlapping spheres model; and (4) classroom or octopus model. You can draw these freehand or prepare an overhead transparency or piece of newsprint. The descriptions that accompany each model are intended as background information for you. Use your own words to talk about them.

As you show each model to the group, ask participants to generate names for each as an opening move in discussing how change

The previous small-group discussion focuses on the different ways in which resource teachers work with colleagues to promote change. In such discussions, participants typically talk about how resource teachers work or what strategies seem more or less successful—comments that emphasize the contextualized nature of the resource teachers' work. In this activity, participants are asked to step back from the work itself in order to reflect on the models for change or the underlying theories that shape the particular ways in which resources teachers or other teacher leaders might work with colleagues. By examining models that are more generic in nature, participants have the opportunity to contemplate the kinds of interactions that promote change. This activity concludes with a discussion that brings together change models and the particularized examples of how resource teachers work. As a facilitator, you will be helping participants move from the specifics of resource teacher work to the general models of change and then back to the specifics of resource teacher work.

Figure 7.1: Telephone Model

As children we might have played the telephone game in which one person whispers a message to the next person, who in turn speaks to the next person and so on. This model presumes that change happens individual by individual, and developing a critical mass is like developing long strings of individuals who have the same information, are committed to the same values, or are implementing the same kinds of reform. The advantages of this method are the individual (and often individualized) contacts that are made and the opportunity to easily revise or update the "message" that is being communicated. The disadvantages of this method are the time needed to communicate with people one by one, and the potential for distortion of the message (as in the children's game of telephone, what the first person says and what the last person hears can be vastly different).

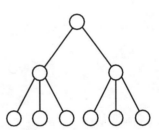

Figure 7.2: Pyramid or Train-the-Trainer Model

A pyramid consists of many layers of teachers or teacher leaders who have responsibility for reaching others. The focus is on how each layer—of stones or teachers—fits with the layers above and below. Multilayered structures, such as stone pyramids, are constructed from the ground up. Multilayered structures, like multiple cadres of teacher leaders, are often implemented from the top down (one person reaches two others; those two each reach two others; those four each reach two others, and so on). Whether stone or human, pyramids are complex constructions. One advantage of the pyramid model is the regularity and symmetry of the layers, so that the work of teacher leaders looks similar. One disadvantage is that the pyramid is only as strong as each of its layers.

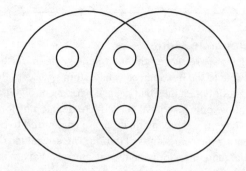

Figure 7.3: Overlapping Spheres Model

In different spheres of professional life, there are many ways in which the work of teacher leaders overlaps. The influence and reach of teacher leaders can be extended by maximizing the places where their work overlaps. For example, other grade-level teachers can learn more about the implications of their efforts for the entire school from a teacher leader who understands both the larger school context for change and the inner workings of a particular grade level. The advantage of this model is that it either utilizes the natural areas of overlap or offers clear, strategic places for increasing the overlap. The disadvantage is that teacher leaders need to be skillful in getting the most out of the overlapping spheres of work by translating what they know from one sphere to the other.

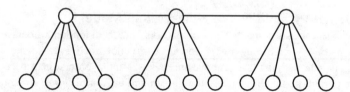

Figure 7.4: Classroom or Octopus Model

In this model, teacher leaders are responsible for working with a number of teachers just as a classroom teacher is responsible for working with a number of students. The numbers may vary, but the premise is that a critical mass develops when one teacher leader is focused on a specific group of colleagues. The advantage is that it limits the teachers that any a single teacher leader works with at a given time to a more manageable number. The disadvantage is that this model can promote the "one stop shopping" approach, which assumes that a teacher leader would be able to meet all their colleagues' needs as they engage in changing their practice.

happens. Then, talk about the how each model operates and the apparent advantages and disadvantages of each.

Consider the following questions:

- What name would you give to this model? Why?
- Can you offer an example of this model from your own experience?
- How does this model operate in terms of reaching large numbers of teachers?
- What advantages does this model have? What disadvantages?

When participants have had the chance to talk about the different change models, connect the discussion to the earlier conversation about developing a critical mass. The intention is to help participants consider a variety of ways to develop a critical mass for change efforts. Ask participants to discuss the following questions:

- How long does it take to develop a critical mass with each of these models?
- Match the scenarios for utilizing teacher leaders with these models. What model for change fits the scenario in which a resource teacher is assigned to each school? Deployed on an "as requested" basis? Assigned to grade levels? Working with targeted populations?
- Return to the recommendations Emily and Abigail made in the role plays. What are their models for change?

Securing Resources and Policy Support

As this case illustrates, there is often a first wave of enthusiastic and committed teacher leaders who get involved in new change efforts. They may be individuals who volunteer for this work, who are recruited because of their past experience, or who "join up" early in the initial stages. However, change efforts succeed only when larger numbers of individuals are involved, and that includes increased numbers of teacher leaders. Some of the first wave of teacher leaders may have to be replaced because they have personal or professional commitments that prevent continued participation. Others may look to new opportunities for continued professional growth. Some may get burned out or disenchanted with the change effort. There is also the need to increase the corps of teacher leaders in order to develop that critical mass for change among teachers.

As Emily, Abigail, and the advisory committee point out, the personal and professional incentives to develop a second wave of teacher leaders can often be different from what brought the first wave in. And if the first wave is perceived to be burned out, it is even more difficult to find teachers for a second wave of leaders.

Small-group discussion (15–20 minutes)

In this activity, participants consider factors that can invite or inhibit a second wave of teacher leaders using the case for brainstorming ideas. Be ready to offer examples of resources (e.g., materials, time, money, personnel) and policies (e.g., professional development access, release time, scheduling). Participants in the small groups should record these factors on newsprint divided into two columns (first wave, second wave) and post their lists for all to see. Pose the following questions as needed:

- What personal or professional incentives might be important to a first wave of teacher leaders? How are these different from the incentives that might be important to a second wave of teacher leaders?
- What district resources or policies need to be mustered to sustain a second wave of teacher leaders? Are these the same as the resources or policies needed to sustain the first wave?

Large-group discussion (15–20 minutes)

The large-group discussion begins with a gallery walk. Participants should look at each group's listing of the factors that inhibit or invite a first and a second wave of teacher leaders. Ask each participant to note one new factor that wasn't on his or her group's original list. After the gallery walk, bring the larger group together for reflection on issues that particularly affect a second wave of teacher leaders. Pose the following questions:

- What factors regarding a second wave of teacher leaders appeared most consistently on the various displays? Why?
- What factors regarding a second wave of teacher leaders were new to you as you looked at the displays? How significant were these new factors?
- Looking back at the whole set of resources and policies affecting a first or second wave, which are most instrumental for developing teacher leaders? For sustaining the work of teacher leaders? Is there a difference? Why?

Imagining Outcomes

Participants will have an opportunity to imagine what the next meeting of the math advisory committee will be like in terms of the recommendation Emily and Abigail bring back to the committee. The activity concludes with a discussion of what the math resource teacher role might look like a year from now, if this recommendation is adopted.

The literature on implementing innovation suggests that teachers will have some predictable concerns as they try to do so. Managerial issues are often foremost, followed by conceptual issues; concerns about collaboration tend to follow later. Such patterns suggest that different incentives for implementing innovations are important to different teachers and depend on their concerns. See Hord et al. (1987) and Loucks-Horsley et al. (1990).

Early adopters of any innovation are often individuals who have prior implementation experience. Because of that previous experience, they may have fewer managerial concerns and be able to move more quickly to consider other kinds of concerns. Or they may feel more comfortable as change agents and be able to sustain greater enthusiasm despite the difficulties. These early adopters of innovation can be like a first wave of teacher leaders—individuals who may have prior leadership experience and therefore fewer managerial concerns, and who are more comfortable seeing themselves as change agents. Like late adopters of innovation, a second wave of teacher leaders may have less experience, more managerial concerns, and feel less comfortable about the change agent role. Expecting a second wave of teacher leaders to act like a first wave is risky, just as it is risky to assume that early and later adopters of any innovation are alike.

Large-group discussion (10–15 minutes)

Brainstorm a list of possible recommendations that Emily and Abigail might make to the advisory committee. Encourage participants not to focus on whether there is agreement between Emily and Abigail or widespread support among committee members. Discuss the recommendations and identify the policies that would be affected. You might use the following questions to prompt discussion:

- What recommendations *might* Emily and Abigail make to the advisory committee?
- What district policies would be affected in some way by each recommendation?

Small-group discussion (15–20 minutes)

Working from the list of recommendations generated by the large group, ask participants to form small groups around each specific recommendation. Each participant should identify the recommendation he or she supports at this time and meet with other like-minded participants. If more than eight people support a particular recommendation, break the group into two smaller groups. If only two people support a particular recommendation, ask that they join their second choice group so that each group has four to five people. Pose the following questions:

- If this recommendation were implemented in the Fairfield Public Schools, how would the situation look a year from now? What implications would this recommendation have for the resource teachers? For classroom teachers? For school or district administrators?
- What policies would have changed, and how would those changes have been made?

Encourage participants to draw on their knowledge from the Fairfield Public Schools case and on their own experiences as educators. There is no right or wrong answer, and no one best recommendation. The purpose is to play out the ramifications of a particular recommendation in order to understand more fully the choices that go into making such a decision.

Large-group discussion (10–20 minutes)

You may choose to bring the small groups back together to share their conversations. Ask each to offer a couple of points from the group's scenario of the situation one year from now. Or ask each group to describe how they imagined changes in policies might be achieved. Or ask each group to identify the affect of the recommendation on resource teachers, classroom teachers, or administrators.

Wrapping Up

This closing activity is designed to help participants arrive at some closure to their work with the case. Adapt the activity described below to fit the case experience you have constructed with participants. How you wrap up the case discussion and what you emphasize will depend on the purpose you have identified for this case experience. In this activity, participants are asked to reflect on issues related to teacher leadership that are prominent at the beginning of a reform initiative and compare them to issues after the reform is up and running.

Individual written reflection (5–10 minutes)

Ask participants to reflect on the following questions and make notes they can use in sharing their ideas in the large group:

- What issues related to teacher leadership do schools, districts, or projects initiating work in school reform typically focus on?
- What teacher leadership issues emerge as a school, district, or project concentrates on sustaining and extending the reform beyond its initial years?
- How are these issues similar and different?

Large-group discussion (10–15 minutes)

Ask participants to share their ideas about the similarities and differences among teacher leadership issues at the outset or during the course of a reform initiative. Your role is to help identify important similarities and differences among the issues. You may choose to begin by discussing and recording participants' ideas about teacher leadership issues at the outset of a reform initiative and follow it with a discussion of teacher leadership issues related to sustaining and extending a reform.

APPENDIX A

Strategies Index

The facilitator's guide in each of the seven chapters in this volume outline many of the same strategies. To encourage you to try new activities and to aid you in finding activities that fit the case experience you are constructing, we have produced this Strategies Index. We have listed below variations of the same activity, for example, all the variations on the "Getting Started" activities or different ways in which you might set up and orchestrate a role play activity. We imagine that you might use this index in different ways.

- Look at all the variations on an activity (such as gathering evidence) to develop an understanding of its intent.
- Consider the variations on an activity (such as reporting to the larger group) to get ideas you can use or adapt in your case experience.
- Compare two variations on an activity (such as reflective writing) to see how it is adapted to fit the goals and the issues of a particular case experience.
- Study one or more variations (such as role playing) to increase your skill at using it well.

Strategy	Page numbers
Getting Started	25, 44, 58, 77, 92, 109, 127
Understanding Perspectives	26, 45, 59, 77, 93, 110, 129
Gathering Evidence	30, 45, 93, 129
Reporting	27, 47, 62, 78, 96, 113, 136
Reflective Writing	28, 50, 65, 82, 98, 114, 131
Role Playing	32, 48, 60, 100, 129
Creating an Artifact	51, 70, 111
Wrapping Up	32, 52, 66, 84, 101, 116, 138

What Leaders Need to Know About School Culture

By understanding the culture existing in schools, linking with the cultural network, meeting teachers' needs, and continually modeling and articulating the emerging vision of the school, leaders can shape the school culture toward continuous improvement.

Joye Hall Norris

A school is more than a building— it is a society and a culture that shapes the learning of staff and students alike. Because that fact is too often ignored, national and state reform efforts have left schools fundamentally unchanged.

For the most part, teachers are doing their best under increasingly difficult circumstances, yet their individual best is no longer good enough. All educators need to understand the cultural constraints that may lead to low performance to examine ways to maximize staff involvement in sustained change. To address these issues, this article provides an overview of school culture, descriptions of school cultures, and seven mechanisms leaders may use to affect the culture of a school.

Joye Hall Norris is an assistant professor, Arizona State University West, Department of Educational Leadership, P.O. Box 37100, Phoenix, AZ 85069-7100, (602) 543-6370.

School Culture

In a general sense, culture refers to the dynamics of a social group and includes the beliefs, values, and practices accepted by the group members. The group operates within a common set of assumptions about the way things are done. Because the culture actually defines what is possible and not possible (Erickson, 1987), people within a culture tend to view issues in a similar manner.

This is as true in schools as it is in society at large. As new teachers become socialized into a school setting, they adopt the common practices of the school.

Schools as Loosely-Coupled Systems

Some organizational cultures are, by nature, strongly binding. These cultures are characterized by a single purpose and, to a great extent, standardized procedures. School cultures, however, have been described as loosely-coupled systems (Weick, 1982) forged in part by teachers' isolation from their peers. Weick (1982) describes loosely-

coupled systems as, "more elusive, less tangible and harder to grasp," than other organizations (p. 675).

Teachers are professionals with recognized subject expertise, which results in different forms of expert power within the school setting. Consequently, administrative practices which are directive in nature or contrary to teachers' beliefs will have little impact on classroom practices, and it is unlikely that meaningful change can be accomplished through administrative command or fiat (Purkey & Smith, 1983).

Contrasting School Cultures

While the culture of schools in general may be defined as loosely coupled, this does not describe the culture of all schools. Many schooling practices are unique and reflect differences in community expectations, beliefs of the founding faculty, and administrative preferences. Often these differences are apparent even to a casual observer. Rosenholtz (1989) found that school cultures varied from building to building and can be placed on a continuum from the highly cohesive "forward-moving" school on one end to "stuck" schools on the other end, in which teacher isolation and estrangement are the norm.

Forward-Moving Schools

Forward-moving schools have growth-oriented values and beliefs supported by all the teachers in the building. These values become the guiding principles used to make decisions and determine educationally-appropriate action. In this healthy system, communication is open as information is shared among all participants, and there is a high level of trust.

Rosenholtz (1989) found that healthy schools are also high-consensus schools and that teacher concern for student academic progress is the focus that prompts teachers to work together, share instructional strategies, and engage in continuous improvement. Teachers in high-consensus schools put aside petty differences to accomplish the goals of the school.

Research describing effective schools (Kritek, 1986) delineates the characteristics of some cohesive, forward-moving schools. These schools were generally characterized by principal leadership which focuses on instruction, a safe and orderly environment, high expectations of students, clearly articulated instructional goals, and monitoring of student progress (Edmonds, 1982).

However, there is a key element missing from the literature: descriptions of the ways the schools achieved these qualities. Lambert (1988) speculates that the correlates of effective schools are merely the "tip of the iceberg" and that the correlate of a "safe and orderly environment," for instance, describes what the school has but that "isn't what make the school effective" (p. 55). Lambert states:

A school in which the staff, working together, examines itself and decides that the reading ability of the students is within their power to change and sets about to design a program to do just that is undoubtedly an effective school. Not because of a strong reading program, but because they possess a set of beliefs that causes them to value the following ideas: self-examination, nondefensiveness, working together, power to effect change, unwillingness to believe that certain students can't learn, effective program design and implementation, continued evaluation, the expectation that their program

School leaders can approach school improvement through cultural change by becoming familiar with the values and beliefs embedded in the school and by shaping the culture in new directions. This is a lengthy process which takes understanding, patience, human relations skills, and the ability to communicate.

will work but may need changes along the way, willingness to work through problems and staff leadership (p. 55).

If healthy school cultures are the key to school success (Lambert, 1988; Rosenholtz, 1989), then faculty consensus and support are instruments of effective cultures and school improvement. The challenge for school leaders is forging a common vision which often requires changing educators' underlying beliefs and attitudes (Purkey & Smith, 1983).

Stuck Schools

According to Rosenholtz (1989), stuck schools are characterized by a lack of consensus on educational goals, teacher isolation, and contrived collegiality. Because education is complex and lacks clear boundaries, there is professional latitude regarding what constitutes teaching and learning. When teachers within a given school are free to define teaching as each sees fit, then they may choose goals which meet their personal needs and preferences (Rosenholtz, 1989). Lack of consensus may also result in competing factions within the school, and groups of teachers may form cliques which engage in ongoing power struggles.

Teacher isolation also creates barriers to a healthy school culture. Since isolated teachers perceive others to be self-reliant, they are reluctant to ask for help. Isolation from others increases uncertainty as teachers feel that they alone are experiencing the doubts and frustrations of teaching. This perception increases the need to avoid self-

disclosure. Fullan and Hargreaves (1990) relate teachers isolation to feelings of powerlessness as teachers strive for safe, risk-free conditions. They describe the situation as follows:

When teachers are afraid to share their ideas and successes for fear of being perceived as blowing their own horns; when teachers are reluctant to tell others of a new idea on the grounds that others might steal it or take credit for it (or on that they did); when teachers, young or old, are afraid to ask for help because they might be perceived as less than competent; when a teacher uses the same approach year after year even though it is not working— all these tendencies shore up the walls of privatism. They limit growth and improvement quite fundamentally, because they limit access to ideas and practices that might offer better ways of doing things. They institutionalize conservatism (p. 39-40).

While teacher isolation and conservatism hamper improvement, another situation called "contrived collegiality" (Hargreaves & Dawe, 1990) can have a similar impact. Contrived collegiality occurs when teachers are placed in a collaborative situation by administrative design for the purpose of implementing standardized processes. Within this context, standardized and centralized school improvement does not allow teachers' voices to be heard. The result is that teachers work together to learn and implement a program with little or no opportunity to discuss the validity or utility of the

Learning the culture of the school is learning how things are done, why they are done in that way, and what happened to the people and institution in the process. Allowing people to share their stories and historical insights provides them with a chance to get feelings and even hostilities out in the open.

The leaders of forward-moving organizations are risktakers, open to the ideas of others, willing to admit to mistakes, trust others to do their job, have a sense of humor, energize others, and believe in continuous improvement.

program within the existing school culture. According to Hargreaves and Dawe (1990):

Cooperative learning, active learning, inductive teaching...are not merely different technical procedures to be selected according to their proven efficiency or inefficiency. They embody particular and disputable educational purposes, they suit teachers with particular kinds of personality and educational beliefs, and they are more appropriate for some contexts than for others. To suppress discussion of these things by drawing in the boundaries of the debate at an early stage and reducing possible disputes about ends to technical discussion over means is to create the conditions for private withdrawal and submerged resistance at a later stage. No amount of standardization will eradicate the meaning and purpose of teaching from those who practice the craft: It will simply drive them underground (p. 236).

Cultural Change

Realistically, how can change be approached in schools when frequently, if not always, the existing culture does not support change? While some educators deal with new initiatives by taking early retirement, others retire on-the-job, and still others choose to fight change. Leaders often become fearful and protective of their domains, or stand back and take a disengaged, wait-and-see posture.

Mechanisms for Shaping School Culture

School leaders can approach school improvement through cultural change by becoming familiar with the values and beliefs embedded in the school and by shaping the culture in new directions. This is a lengthy

process which takes understanding, patience, human relations skills, and the ability to communicate. Changing the culture involves changing habits of mind, body, and spirit and involves the following processes:

1. *Learn the Existing Culture.* Study the culture of a school in terms of heroes and heroines, areas of pride, rituals, ceremonies, and cultural networks (Deal & Kennedy, 1982). Heroes and heroines are persons revered for their accomplishments and contributions to the school and exemplify the values of the school. Rituals are the routines of school life that establish boundaries of acceptable behavior, and ceremonies provide concrete examples of what is valued. In order to enter the cultural network, learn the role that various people play in shaping, interpreting, and supporting the culture of the organization. To learn about the culture and key people, ask questions about the meanings behind events and why things are done the way they are.

Deal and Kennedy (1982) recommend asking people who relate stories about the organization for the names of others who could share additional information. Establish a relationship with the key people who can explain events and provide insights. Get the story tellers' perspectives on past change initiatives, a description of the change process, level of success, and current feelings regarding the changes. These stories are likely to provide insight into areas where change approaches have caused institutional resistance.

Learning the culture of the school is learning how things are done, why they are done in that way, and what happened to the people and institution in the process. Allowing people to share their stories and historical insights provides them with a chance to get

feelings and even hostilities out in the open.

2. *Establish Communication Linkages.* Tapping into the formal and informal communication system of the organization provides understanding of the current culture and can help create new cultural realities. Feel the pulse of the organization through informal conversations, feedback surveys, suggestion boxes, spontaneous interviews, and an open-door policy. People at all levels of the organization can be key players in providing communication linkages to the broader community.

For instance, change agents need to remember the vital role that secretaries play in interpreting the cultural change for staff. Secretaries have a unique vantage point with close proximity to leadership teams and often have longevity within the institution. They are in a position to observe the intent and actions of leadership and can calm group fears or fuel them.

3. *Meet Teacher Needs.* Because of the complex, non-routine nature of teaching, teacher social and psychological well being is often threatened by change (Rosenholtz, 1989). To combat this, leaders can provide teachers with a sense of achievement by documenting the accomplishments of the school. One leadership team begins each school year describing the history of the school improvement efforts from inception. This allows participants to reflect and appreciate their progress.

One principal enhances teacher self-esteem by providing the resources and encouragement necessary for every teacher to be the in-house expert on a facet of education. Teachers need to know that their efforts are noticed and appreciated by others (Rosenholtz, 1989). Simple acknowledgements can go a long way toward making staff feel valued. Rewarding faculty activities compatible with the vision for the school provides incentives to continue.

4. *Create Opportunities for Renewal.* A learning organization is possible only when its individual members are learners (Senge, 1990). Leaders who create opportunities for individual growth recognize that teachers' well being and learning have a direct bearing on student learning. Enlarging the role of professional development to encompass areas of personal renewal and reflection shows respect for teachers and promotes good mental health, which is essential in healthy organizations.

Encouraging teachers to accept chal-

School leaders model the vision that they have for the school. If the vision includes teachers sharing power with students and parents, then leaders must be willing to share power with teachers.

lenges such as teaching a different grade or course, teaching other teachers, organizing staff development programs, or seeking external funding for their ideas creates avenues for growth and self-actualization. Little (1990) supports the concept of "joint work" which allows teachers to work together on common problems related to their jobs. Through truly collaborate ventures, teachers can gain technical knowledge, appreciate the complexity of the job as others share their problems, and increase their esprit de corps.

5. *Practice Leadership.* The role of leadership is to build a strong culture which is open to self-examination and innovation. Promoting a learning community where the principal is the number one learner can set the stage. One principal, for example, might buy 10 copies of educationally-relevant books for teachers to read and host after school meetings to discuss the new ideas. The constant infusion of ideas and the opportunity to share insights with peers can change the belief system of a school.

A leader needs to question current practice and determine if there are more creative ways to approach the issue. The leaders of forward-moving organizations are risktakers, open to the ideas of others, willing to admit to mistakes, trust others to do their jobs, have a sense of humor, energize others, and believe in continuous improvement.

6. *Model Desired Behaviors.* School leaders model the vision that they have for the school. If the vision includes teachers sharing power with students and parents, then leaders must be willing to share power with teachers. If the vision includes a learning environment for all persons involved with education, then principals must focus on adult learning as well as student learning.

7. *Hire the Right People.* As school leadership has the opportunity to hire new faculty, a match between school vision and individual philosophy is critical (Purkey & Smith, 1983; Rosenholtz, 1989). Schools with a well articulated set of beliefs must recruit people who support this orientation or the school will not move forward. Districts need to pay attention to teacher recruitment and the selection process. Last minute or hurried hiring practices need to be replaced by screening processes which assess the values and educational beliefs of candidates as well as their teaching skills. The school must determine if the candidate can work with others to create a community of learners, is flexible, views issues through multiple perspectives, deals with ambiguity, and sees his or her own learning as life-long.

Conclusion

The culture of schools greatly influences what types of changes and the degree to which change may occur within a given school. Leaders need to be aware of pervasive cultural aspects of schools, such as lack of consensus, teacher isolation, and contrived collegiality, that are barriers to school improvement.

Leaders need to understand that they are shapers of school culture. By understanding the existing culture, linking with the cultural network, meeting teachers' needs, and continually modeling and articulating the emerging vision of the school, leaders can shape the school culture toward continuous improvement.

References

Deal, T.E., & Kennedy, A.A. (1982) *Corporate cultures.* Reading, MA: Addison-Wesley.

Edmonds, R.R. (1982). Programs for school improvement: An overview. *Phi Delta Kappan, 64*(4), 4-11.

Erickson, F. (1987). Conceptions of school culture: An overview. *Educational Administration Quarterly, 23*(4), 11-24.

Fullan, M.G., & Hargreaves, A. (1990). *What's worth fighting for? Working together for your school.* Andover, MA: The Regional Laboratory for Education Improvement of the Northwest and Islands.

Hargreaves, A., & Dawe, R. (1990). Paths of professional development: Contrived collegiality, collaborative culture, and the case of peer coaching. *Teaching & Teacher Education, 6*(3), 227-241.

Kritek, W.J. (1986, April). *School culture and school improvement.* Paper presented at the annual meeting of the American Educational Research Association, San Francisco, CA.

Lambert, L.G. (1988). Building school culture: An open letter to principals. *NASSP Bulletin, 72*(506), 54-62.

Little, J.W. (1990). The persistence of privacy: Autonomy and initiative in teachers' professional relations. *Teachers College Record, 91*(4), 509-536.

Purkey, S.C., & Smith, M.S. (1983). Effective schools: A review. *The Elementary School Journal, 83*(4), 427-452.

Rosenholtz, S.J. (1989). *Teachers' workplace.* New York: Longman.

Senge, P.M. (1990). *The fifth discipline: The art and practice of the learning organization.* New York: Doubleday/Currency.

Weick, K.E. (1982). Administering education in loosely coupled schools. *Phi Delta Kappan, 63*(10), 673-676.

The ExxonMobil Foundation

The Exxon Corporation created the Exxon Education Foundation in 1955 to strengthen education in the United States, particularly higher education. In 1999, when Exxon Corporation and Mobil Corporation merged, the Exxon Education Foundation was renamed the ExxonMobil Foundation. Since 1955, the Foundation has given more than $500 million in support of American education.

Today, the ExxonMobil Foundation's principal areas of interest are:

- Mathematics education, especially at the primary grades
- Reform of undergraduate science, technology, engineering, and mathematics teaching and learning
- K–12 science education
- Teacher education
- Effective assessment strategies at all levels of education
- Increased educational opportunities for minorities in the mathematics, science, and engineering disciplines

The principles that have consistently guided the Foundation were set out in its first report in 1955: "In the conviction that business organizations must do all they can to ensure growth and strength of the nation's educational institutions [Exxon] and its affiliates intend to continue to search for the most effective and appropriate ways to lend such support. The [Exxon] Education Foundation provides a permanent organization to implement that support."

While remaining true to the beliefs set out in 1955, the ExxonMobil Foundation has over time and will in the future, shift its emphasis to reflect changing educational needs. Moreover, grant making has been guided by principles of stewardship that seek to maximize limited funding capacity. The Foundation's Mathematics Education Program, begun in 1987, is a programmatic example of the Foundation's commitment to joining stewardship with national educational need. In

1987, the Foundation's Trustees approved a new program aimed at improving mathematics education. That decision was made with the understanding that the Foundation should work at this task for at least a decade.

Since 1987 the Foundation has deliberately chosen to address, with the Mathematics Program, a limited set of goals:

- To support the work of key professional organizations in the mathematics and mathematics education community
- To support research and planning aimed at developing a healthy public, university, and school policy environment for improved mathematics instruction
- To improve mathematics teaching in undergraduate settings
- To support the use of mathematics specialists in the primary grades

With these four goals in mind, the Foundation has awarded grants to the National Council of Teachers of Mathematics, the Mathematical Association of America, the Association for Women in Mathematics, the Conference Board of the Mathematical Science, the Joint Policy Board for Mathematics, and the American Mathematical Association of Two-Year Colleges. The Foundation has been a key supporter as well of the National Alliance of State Science and Mathematics Coalitions. In all cases, consistent and often long-term support has helped these national groups to move forward to develop a strong vision of mathematics across all educational levels and to address the increasing diversity among learners in our country.

Likewise, the Foundation has made a significant contribution to primary teachers and students across the United States through the K–3 Mathematics Specialist Program. The overall goal is to allow schools and school districts to develop a mathematics specialist role that best fits the needs of local situations. To this end, grant funds are generally applied to ongoing professional development of teachers and specialists as they seek to strengthen their own knowledge of mathematics, knowledge of children's mathematical thinking, new curricular materials, theories of learning, and instructional and assessment strategies. The ExxonMobil Foundation has also help to launch some of the more innovative professional development initiatives in elementary mathematics, such as the *Developing Mathematical Ideas* leadership institutes, as well as several projects connected with the Freudenthal Institute.

From the inception of the K–3 Program the Foundation has provided a network of resources for specialists and project teachers. A designated Project Facilitator and Program Advisor have served as liaisons to project sites. A Program newsletter, "Intersection," an electronic mail listserve known as "Exxon Teachers Networking with

Teachers" (ExxonTNT), and an annual meeting for project directors and specialists are core network pieces that work in tandem to facilitate information sharing and active communications among project sites.

The Foundation also has had a long-standing role in supporting two of the more visible national educational initiatives—the work of Ted Sizer and the Coalition of Essential Schools and the National Network for Educational Renewal under the leadership of John Goodlad. More recent support of national projects has gone to the work of a growing network of newly graduated mathematics Ph.D.'s through Project NeXT (New Experiences in Teaching) and to Project Kaleidoscope's Faculty for the 21st Century. The Foundation has also played a key role in advancing the work of mathematics faculty in community colleges through support for the American Mathematics Association for Two-Year Colleges (AMATYC).

The ExxonMobil Foundation will continue to play an active role in American education. This work will be guided, as it has in the past, by an ongoing belief that it is educational institutions at all levels that shape the country's human resources, creating the foundation for a higher standard of learning and a better quality of life for everyone.

The Merck Institute for Science Education

To help ensure that all children receive a good science education, Merck & Co., Inc. created the Merck Institute for Science Education (MISE) in 1993. MISE's mission is to improve students' performance and participation in science during the formative years of kindergarten through eighth grade. To accomplish this mission, the Institute has three primary goals:

- deepening current and future teachers' knowledge of science and education;
- providing access to exemplary curriculum materials; and
- supporting policies at the local, state, and national levels that promote science education.

During its first years of operation, the Institute focused its efforts on school districts in New Jersey and Pennsylvania, where Merck has its major operations. MISE works closely with the faculty, administration, and community leaders in these districts to enhance science education in elementary and middle schools. Once the Institute's goals have been achieved in these initial partner districts, the Institute will replicate its programs in other districts. In 1995, the Institute was awarded a five-year, $2.4 million National Science Foundation grant under NSF's Local Systemic Change program. The award has enabled the Institute and its partners to expand and intensify their work.

The first of MISE's three goals, deepening teachers' knowledge of science, is crucial to improving student performance in science. Equally important is strengthening expertise in how to teach science. Providing teachers with opportunities to build this strong foundation of science knowledge and teaching skills is an Institute priority. The Institute's professional development programs focus on K–8 schools near Merck's largest facilities. Working closely with teachers, curriculum supervisors, and administrators in these districts, the Institute helps to improve the teaching and learning of science through programs focused on inquiry-centered learning.

There are three main programs that form the core of the Institute's professional development program. The Leader Teacher Institute is one program that aims to build a team of teachers grounded in inquiry-centered learning and capable of leading science reform in their schools and districts. This three-year program deepens teachers' science knowledge, strengthens their teaching practice, and builds their leadership skills. Through inquiry, teachers learn science by doing science and use this experience to transform science learning in their classrooms and schools.

Peer Teacher Workshops is another professional development program. These workshops complement the Leader Teacher Institute by focusing specifically on districts' science curricula. Designed and facilitated by experts in science education and Leader Teachers, these one-week workshops target specific grade levels and immerse teachers in science investigations directly related to the classroom curriculum.

A third professional development program is the Merck Fellow program. The Institute's professional development reaches future teachers by pairing them with Leader Teachers in a mentorship program. Merck Fellows participate in summer workshops to deepen their experiences with science education. During the following school year, Fellows work in their mentors' classrooms to create and teach science lessons, experiencing the challenges and rewards of the inquiry-centered classroom.

MISE also has the goal of providing access to exemplary curriculum materials in order to enhance the learning environment. Teachers need access to standards-based curricula and teaching materials as well as support from school- and district-level administration, parents, and the community. The Institute addresses these needs through resource centers, Merck employee volunteers, and parent involvement.

Finally, MISE acts on its third goal by promoting policies that support science education at the local, state, and national levels. At the local level, MISE develops leaders through partnerships with targeted school districts in New Jersey and Pennsylvania, and collaborates with school districts in their development of K–8 science education frameworks. MISE works at the state level to influence science education reform through leadership on the New Jersey Science Curriculum Standards Committee and the New Jersey Professional Teaching Standards Board, and provides leadership to several statewide National Science Foundation-funded projects. At the national level, MISE partners with educational organizations to develop curriculum and assessment tools, advocates business-education collaborations, and creates model professional development programs for teachers and administrators.

Bibliography

Action Design Associates. 1996. *Organizational Learning in Action.* Weston, MA: Action Design Associates.

Barnes, L., A. Hansen, and C. R. Christensen. 1994. *Teaching and the Case Method: Text, Cases and Readings.* Boston: Harvard Business School Press.

Barnett, C. 1998. "Mathematics Teaching Cases as a Catlayst for Informed Strategic Inquiry." *Teaching and Teacher Education* 14: 81–93.

Barnett, C., D. Goldenstein, and B. Jackson. 1994. *Fractions, Decimals, Ratios, and Percents: Hard to Teach and Hard to Learn* and *Facilitator's Discussion Guide.* Portsmouth, NH: Heinemann.

Block, P. 1987. *The Empowered Manager.* San Francisco: Jossey-Bass.

Carter, K. 1999. "What Is a Case? What Is Not a Case?" In *Who Learns What from Cases and How? The Research Base for Teaching and Learning with Cases,* ed. M. Lundeberg, B. Levin, and H. Harrington, 165–175. Mahwah, NJ: Erlbaum.

Center for Science Education (CSE) at Education Development Center & Division of Elementary, Secondary and Informal Education (ESIE) at National Science Foundation. 1997. *Foundations: The Challenge of K–8 Science Education Reform.* Vol. 1. Newton, MA: Education Development Center.

Center on Evaluation, Development, and Research. 1989. *Teacher Peer Coaching.* Bloomington, IN: Phi Delta Kappan.

Colbert, J., P. Desberg, and K. Trimbel. 1996. *The Case for Education: Contemporary Approaches for Using Case Methods.* Needham Heights, MA: Allyn & Bacon.

Darling-Hammond, L., and D. Ball. 1998. *Teaching for High Standards: What Policymakers Need to Know and Be Able to Do.* JRE-04. New York: National Commission on Teaching and America's Future and the Consortium for Policy Research in Education.

Fisher, R., and W. Ury. 1991. *Getting to Yes: How to Negotiate Agreement Without Giving In*. New York: Penguin.

Fullan, M. 1993. *Change Forces*. Philadelphia: Falmer Press.

———. 1997. *What's Worth Fighting for in the Principalship?* New York: Teachers College Press.

———. 1999. *Change Forces: The Sequel*. Philadelphia: Falmer Press.

Fullan, M., with S. Stiegelbauer. 1991. *The New Meaning of Educational Change*. New York: Teachers College Press.

Garmston, R. 1993. *Becoming a State-of-the-Art-Presenter: Practical Techniques to Achieve Maximum Results with Adult Audiences*. Bellevue, WA: Bureau of Education and Research.

Garmston, R., and A. Costa. 1994. *Cognitive Coaching: A Foundation for Renaissance Schools*. Norwood, MA: Christopher Gordon.

Garmston, R., and B. Wellman. 1998. "Teacher Talk That Makes a Difference." *Educational Leadership* 55 (7): 30–34.

Hawkins, D. 1974. *The Informed Vision: Essays on Learning and Human Nature*. New York: Agathon Press.

Hord, S., W. Rutherford, L. Huling-Austin, and G. Hall. 1987. *Taking Charge of Change*. Alexandria, VA: Association for Supervision and Curriculum Development.

Joyce, B., and B. Showers, 1988. *Student Achievement Through Staff Development*. White Plains, NY: Longman Inc.

Kleinfeld, J. 1996. "Our Hero Comes of Age: What Students Learn from Case Writing in Student Teaching." In *The Case for Education: Contemporary Approaches for Using Case Methods*, ed. J. Colbert, P. Desberg, and K. Trimbel, 79–94. Needham Heights, MA: Allyn & Bacon.

Koch, L. C. 1997. "The Growing Pains of Change: A Case Study of a Third-Grade Teacher." *Journal for Research in Mathematics Education* 8: 87–107.

Laframboise, K., and P. Griffith. 1997. "Using Literature Cases to Examine Diversity Issues with Preservice Teachers." *Teaching and Teacher Education* 13: 369–382.

Lambert, L. 1998. *Building Leadership Capacity in Schools*. Alexandria, VA: Association for Supervision and Curriculum Development.

Levin, B. 1999. "The Role of Discussion in Case Pedagogy: Who Learns What? And How?" In *Who Learns What from Cases and How? The Research Base for Teaching and Learning with Cases*, ed. M. Lundeberg, B. Levin, and H. Harrington, 139–157. Mahwah, NJ: Erlbaum.

Lieberman, A., and M. Grolnick. 1999. "Networks and Reform in American Education." In *Teaching as the Learning Profession: Handbook of Policy and Practice*, ed. L. Darling-Hammond and G. Sykes, 292–312. San Francisco: Jossey-Bass.

Lieberman, A., E. Saxl, and M. Miles. 1988. "Teacher Leadership: Ideology and Practice." In *Building a Professional Culture in Schools*, ed. A. Lieberman, 149–166. New York: Teachers College Press.

Little, J. W. 1993. "Teachers' Professional Development in a Climate of Educational Reform." *Educational Evaluation and Policy Analysis* 15 (2): 129–151.

Lord, B. 1994. "Teachers' Professional Development: Critical Colleagueship and the Role of Professional Communities." In *The Future of Education: Perspectives on National Standards in Education*, ed. N. Cobb, 175–204. New York: The College Board.

Lord, B., and B. Miller. 2000. *Teacher Leadership: An Appealing and Inescapable Force in School Reform?* Newton, MA: Education Development Center.

Loucks-Horsley, S., P. Hewson, N. Love, and K. Stiles. 1998. *Designing Professional Development for Teachers of Science and Mathematics.* Thousand Oak, CA: Corwin Press.

Loucks-Horsley, S., R. Kapitan, M. Carlson, P. Kuerbis, R. Clark, G. Melle, T. Sachse, and E. Walton. 1990. *Elementary School Science for the 90's.* Alexandria, VA: Association for Supervision and Curriculum Development.

Loucks-Horsley, S., K. Stiles, and P. Hewson. 1996. *Principles of Effective Professional Development for Mathematics and Science Education: A Synthesis of Standards.* Madison: University of Wisconsin at Madison, National Institute for Science Education.

Lundeberg, M., B. Levin, and H. Harrington. 1999. *Who Learns What from Cases and How? The Research Base for Teaching and Learning with Cases.* Mahwah, NJ: Erlbaum.

McGonagill, G. 1995. Private correspondence.

Merseth, K. 1996. "Cases and the Case Method in Teacher Education." In *Handbook of Research on Teacher Education*, ed. J. Sikula, 722–746. New York: Simon & Schuster/Macmillan.

Miller, B., and I. Kantrov. 1998a. *A Guide to Facilitating Cases in Education.* Portsmouth, NH: Heinemann.

———. 1998b. *Casebook on School Reform.* Portsmouth, NH: Heinemann.

Miller, B., and J. Mark. 1995. *Research on Teacher Leadership in Mathematics and Science Education.* Newton, MA: Education Development Center.

Moller, G., and M. Katzenmeyer. 1996. "The Promise of Teacher Leadership." In *Every Teacher as a Leader: Realizing the Potential of Teacher Leadership*, ed. G. Moller and M. Katzenmeyer, 1–17. San Francisco: Jossey-Bass.

Moon, J., and G. Hein. 1995. *Journeys in Change: Lessons from the Field.* Cambridge, MA: Lesley College.

Norris, J. 1994. "What Leaders Need to Know About School Culture." *Journal of Staff Development* 15 (2): 2–5.

Palmer, P. 1998. *The Courage to Teach: Exploring the Inner Landscape of a Teacher's Life.* San Francisco: Jossey-Bass.

Regional Educational Laboratories. 1995. *Facilitating Systemic Change in Science and Mathematics Education: A Toolkit for Professional Developers.* Andover, MA: The Regional Laboratory for Educational Improvement of the Northeast and Islands.

Robbins, P. 1991. *How to Plan and Implement a Peer Coaching Program.* Alexandria, VA: Association for Supervision and Curriculum Development.

Schlechty, P. 1991. *Schools for the 21st Century.* San Francisco: Jossey-Bass.

Sebring, P., and A. Bryk. 1998. *School Leadership and the Bottom Line in Chicago.* Chicago: University of Chicago, Consortium on School Research.

Shulman, J. 1992. Introduction. In *Case Methods in Teacher Education*, ed. J. Shulman, xiii–xvii. New York: Teachers College Press.

———. 1996. "Tender Feelings, Hidden Thoughts: Confronting Bias, Innocence and Racism Through Case Discussions." In *The Case for Education: Contemporary Approaches for Using Case Methods*, ed. J. Colbert, P. Desberg, and K. Trimbel, 137–158. Needham Heights, MA: Allyn & Bacon.

Shulman, L. 1996. "Just in Case: Reflections on Learning from Experience." In *The Case for Education: Contemporary Approaches for Using Case Methods*, ed. J. Colbert, P. Desberg, and K. Trimbel, 197–217. Needham Heights, MA: Allyn & Bacon.

Smylie, M., and J. Brownlee-Conyers. 1992. "Teacher Leaders and Their Principals." *Education Administration Quarterly* 28 (2): 150–184.

St. John, M., J. Century, F. Tibbitts, and B. Heenan. 1994. *Reforming Elementary Science Education in Urban Districts.* Inverness, CA: Inverness Research Associates.

Sykes, G., and T. Bird. 1992. "Teacher Education and the Case Idea." *Review of Research in Education* 18: 457–521.

Webb, N., D. Heck, and W. Tate. 1996. "The Urban Mathematics Collaboratives Project: A Study of Teacher, Community and Reform." In *Bold Ventures*, vol. 3 of *Case Studies of U.S. Innovations in Mathematics Education*, ed. S. Raizen and E. Britton, 245–360. Boston: Kluwer Academic Publishers.

Weiss, I., G. Gellatly, D. Montgomery, C. Ridgway, C. Templeton, and D. Whittington. 1999. *Executive Summary of the Local Systemic Change Through Teacher Enhancement: Year Four Cross-Site Report.* Chapel Hill, NC: Horizon Research, Inc.